ZOMBIE MANGA
COLORING BOOK

A GRUESOME UNDEAD MANGA
COLORING ADVENTURE FOR ADULTS

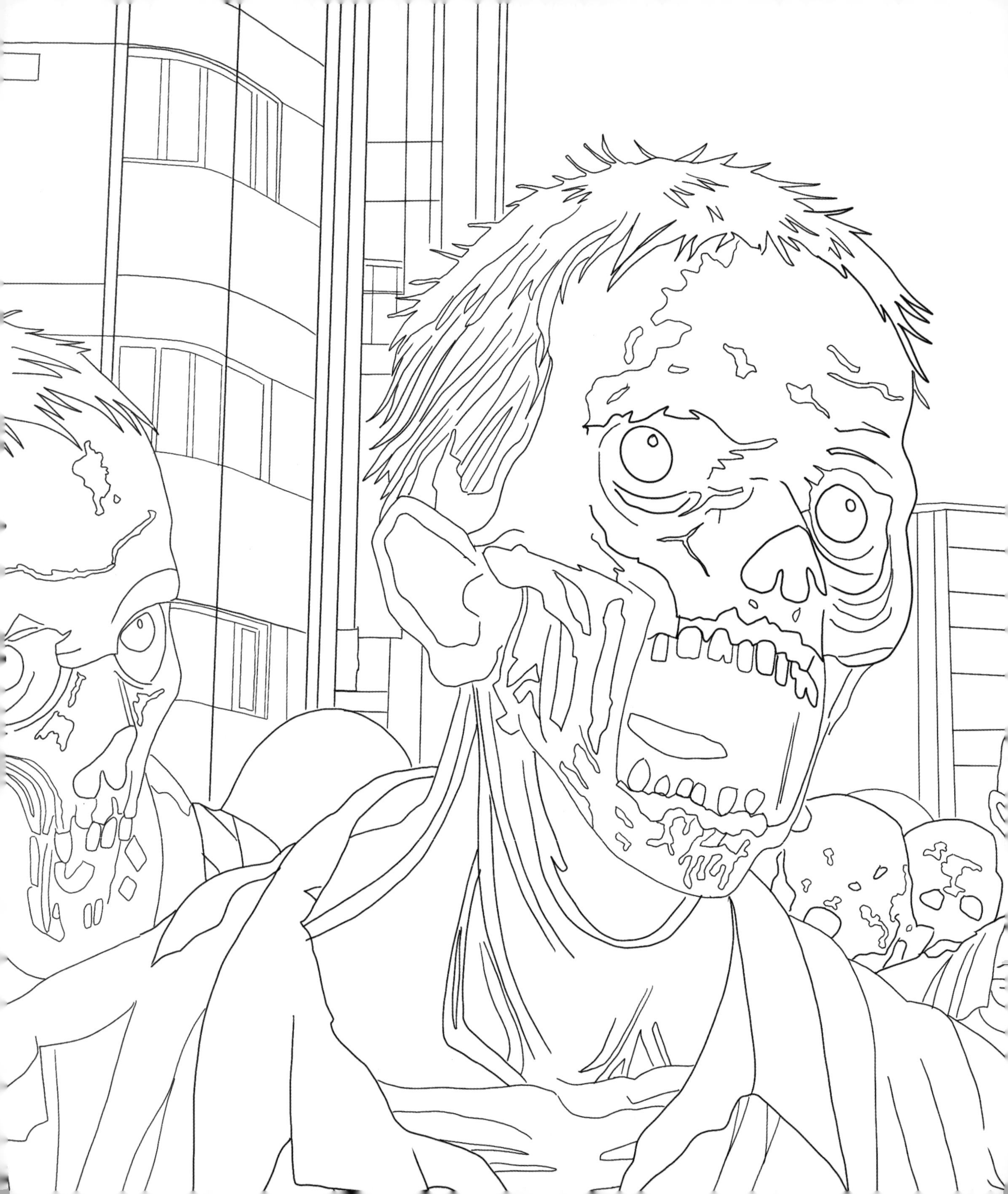

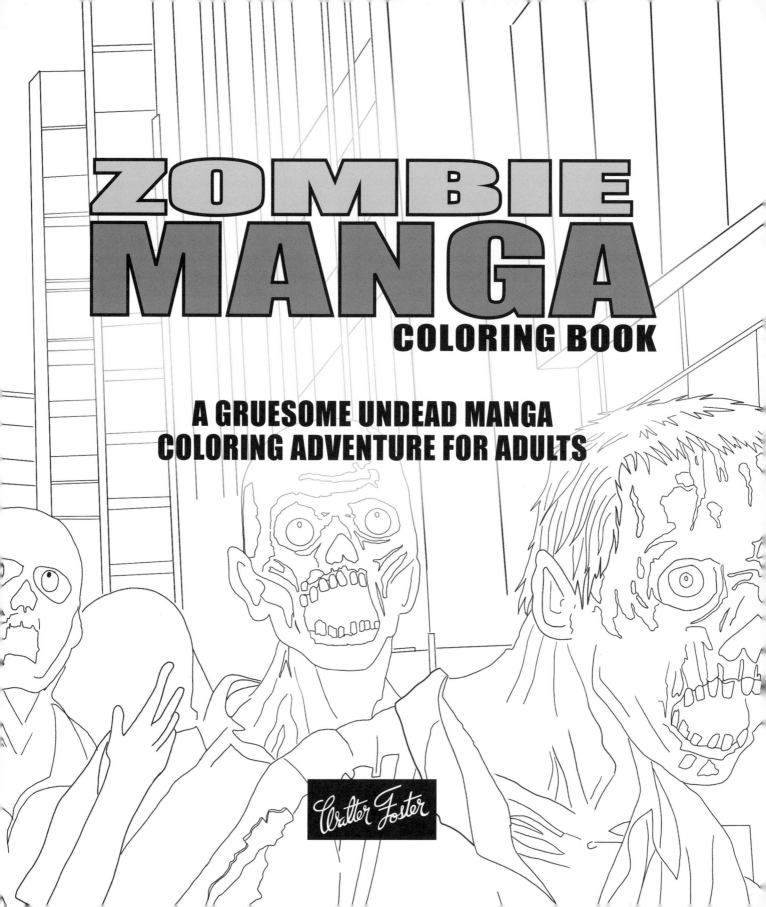

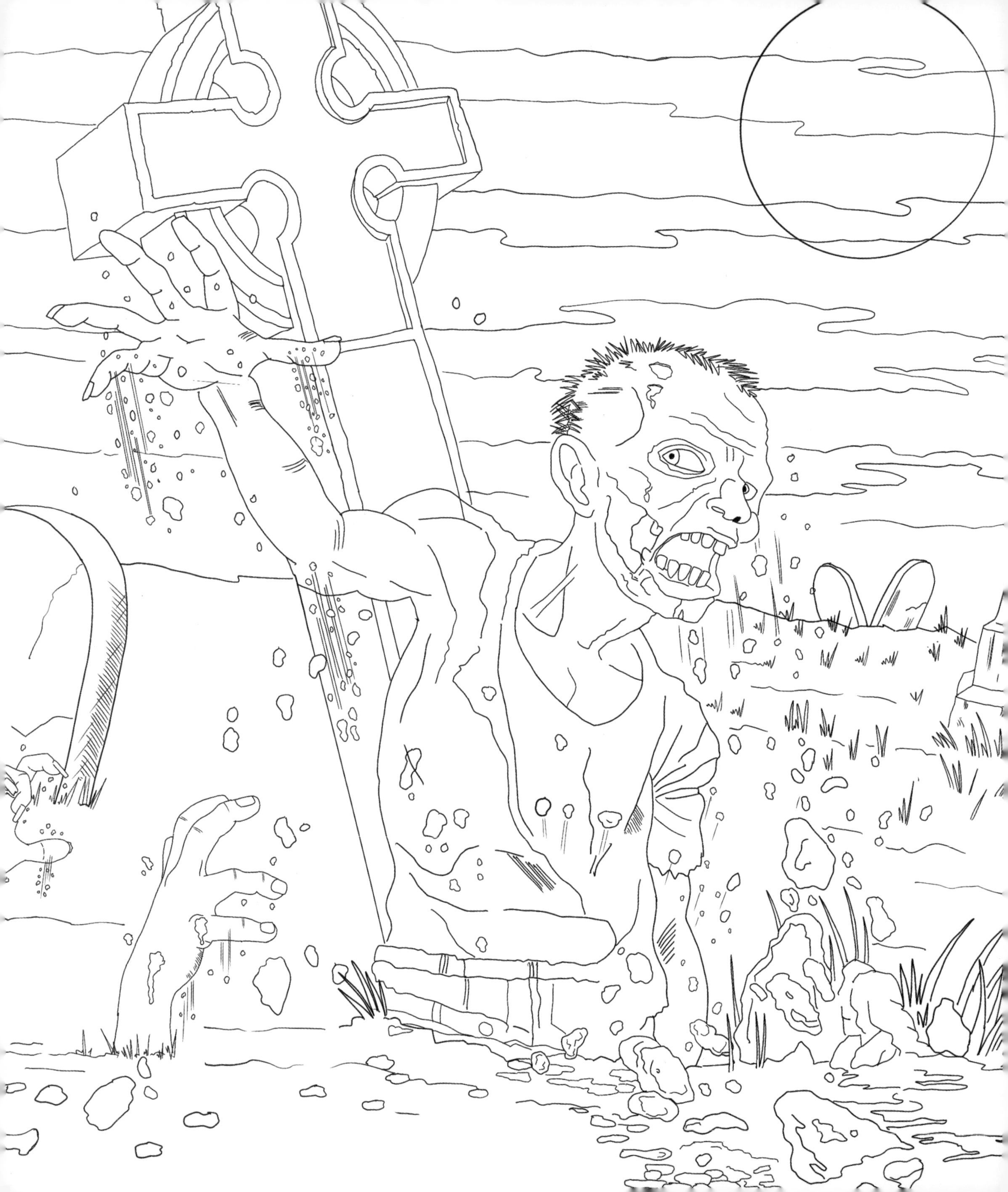

TAKE A CHILLING JOURNEY INTO THE ZOMBIE APOCALYPSE...

Meditation or contemplation is often a very serious challenge—sitting quietly and stress-free in today's busy, noisy environment can be difficult. Channeling your thoughts with an activity such as coloring is far more effective. And what better way to calm the mind than with zombie hoards, severed limbs, maggot infestations, and more! Put your coloring skills (and your love of all things undead) to good use with the *Zombie Manga Coloring Book*.

To make the most of coloring, find a quiet spot where you won't be disturbed (use some headphones if you wish), and lay out your pencils or markers. Think through every stroke and focus on your breathing as you bring to life a variety of manga characters and gruesome scenes. From flesh-eating zombies and splattered brains to action-packed zombie manga attacks and battles, these horrific coloring pages are ready to challenge and inspire your creativity!

How to Use This Book

Pencils are the most versatile medium for coloring, allowing you to mix and blend colors easily, and they won't show through the page. Watercolor pencils create soft backgrounds and a more painterly effect as the colors flow into each other. Markers or gel pens provide more vivid color and can help create outlines, shadows, and highlights. Be careful not to "muddy" the colors with too many layers. Also, try not to press too hard as the color may show through the page.

Use the practice pages at the beginning of the book to try out your coloring techniques and explore different color combinations. This is also a great opportunity to test your pencils and pens to make sure they won't bleed through the paper. Don't worry too much if you go over the lines, there is no right or wrong way to color—and mistakes can sometimes add to the overall atmosphere of your finished piece of artwork.

How to Use This Book

Use the practice pages to try out different techniques and color combinations—be creative!

For dramatic blood effects, try using three or more shades of red. Experiment with greens, blues, and purples. Remember to leave highlights for dimension.

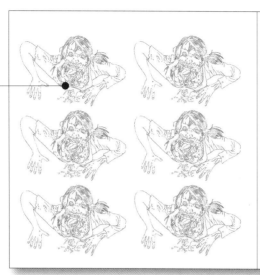 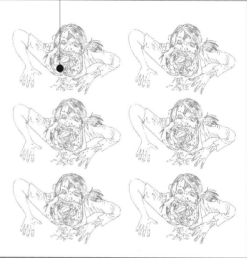

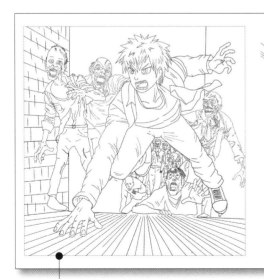 

Some of the coloring pages go all the way to the edge. Try drawing your own frame around a particular area, and then use lighter shades to create a "vignette."

You can add as many frames as you like—creating your own boundaries for different styles, colors, or hues.

Some of the coloring pages have a frame. Try adding a unique border or continue the drawing to the edge of the page.

Some pages don't have a complete background. You can use a solid color or gradient, add to the drawing, or focus your attention on the scene itself.

The lines on the zombie clothes are guides for tears, bloodstains, or flesh wounds underneath. You decide!

The zombies in the background have less detail. You can add in your own or simply add shading to blend them into the scene.

Most pages are left for you to decide whether to soften or continue coloring around the edges. There are no particular rules to follow—try mixing and matching different ideas and techniques.

It doesn't matter if you go over the lines—this is your book to color as you like. Sometimes, mistakes can inspire you to use a new technique!

Practice Pages

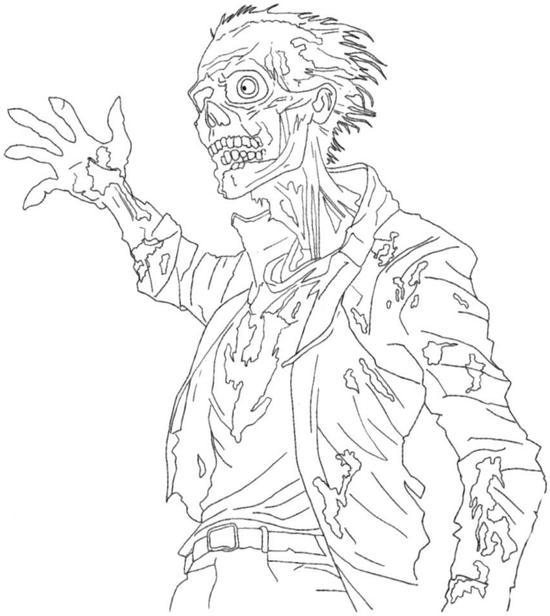

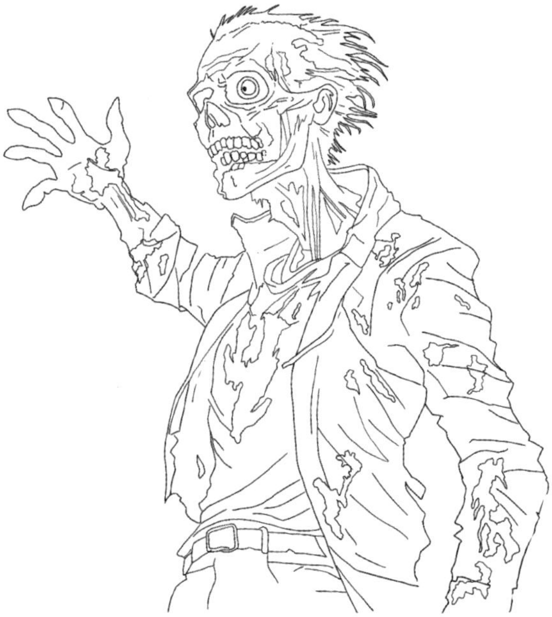

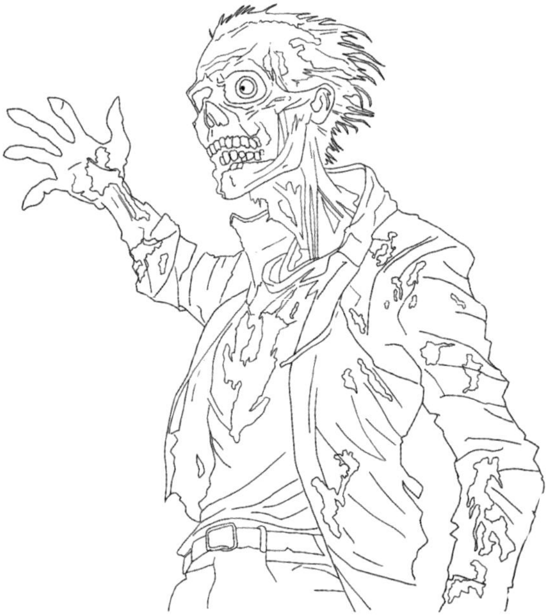

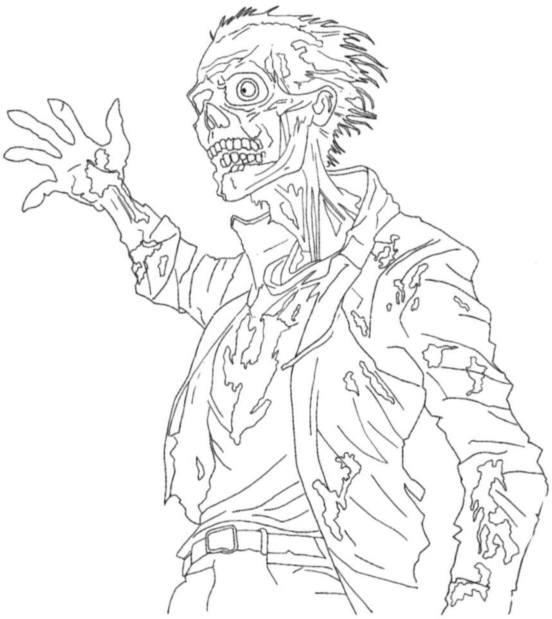

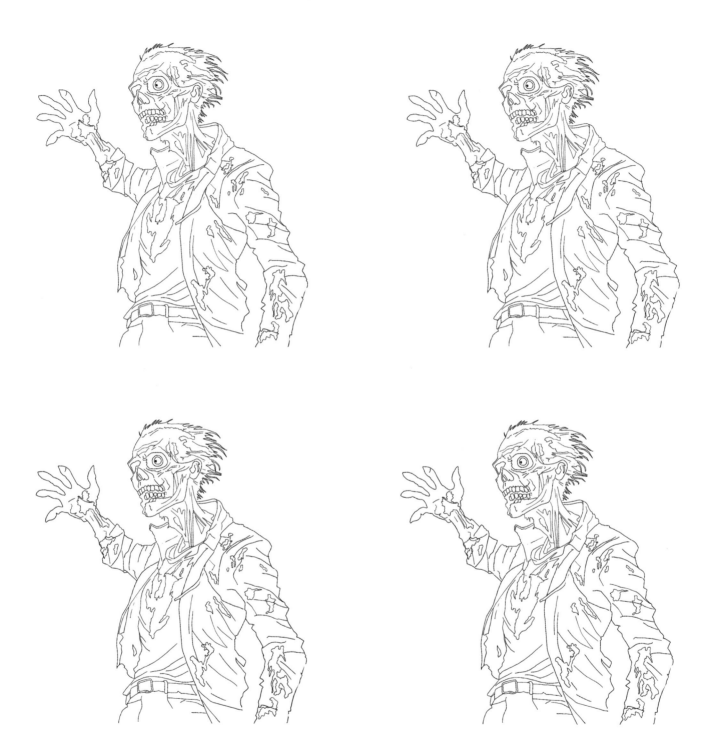

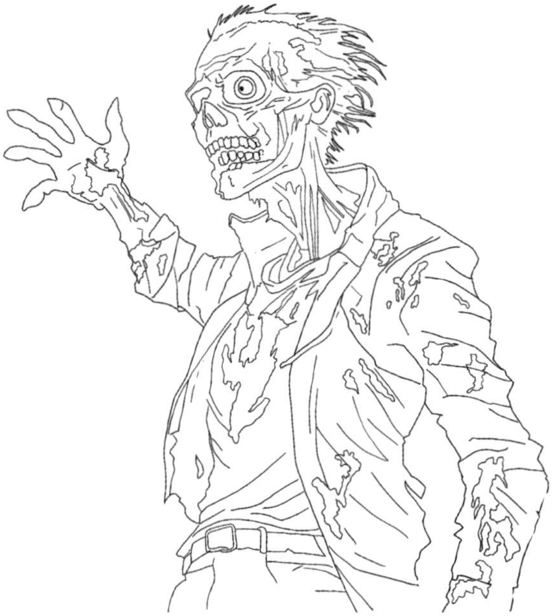

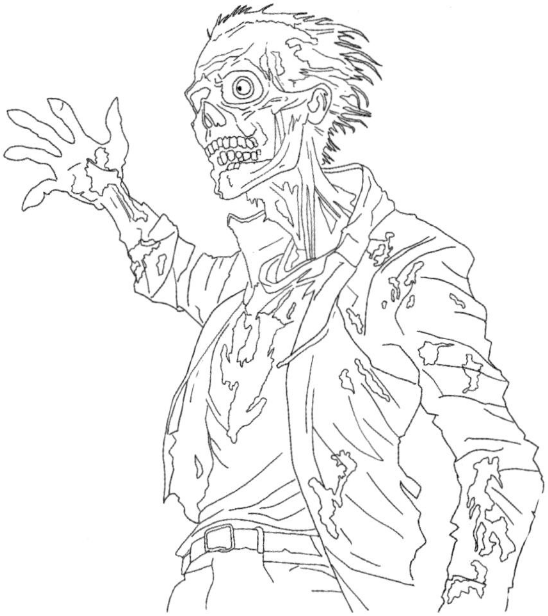

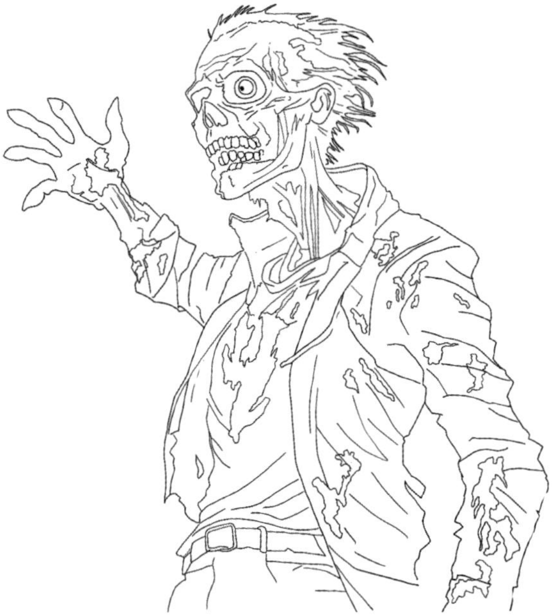

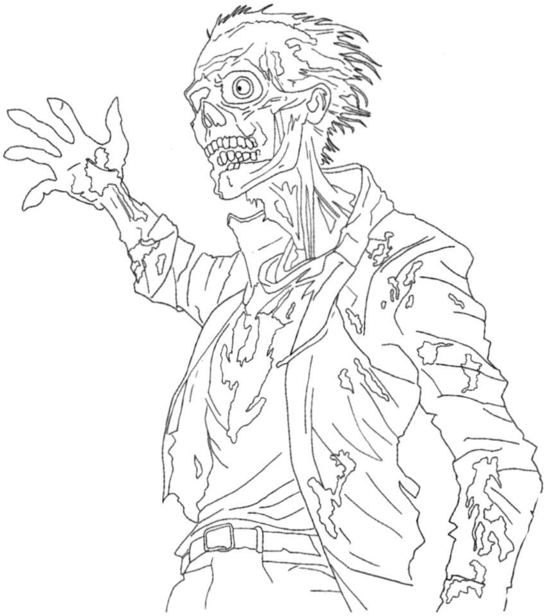

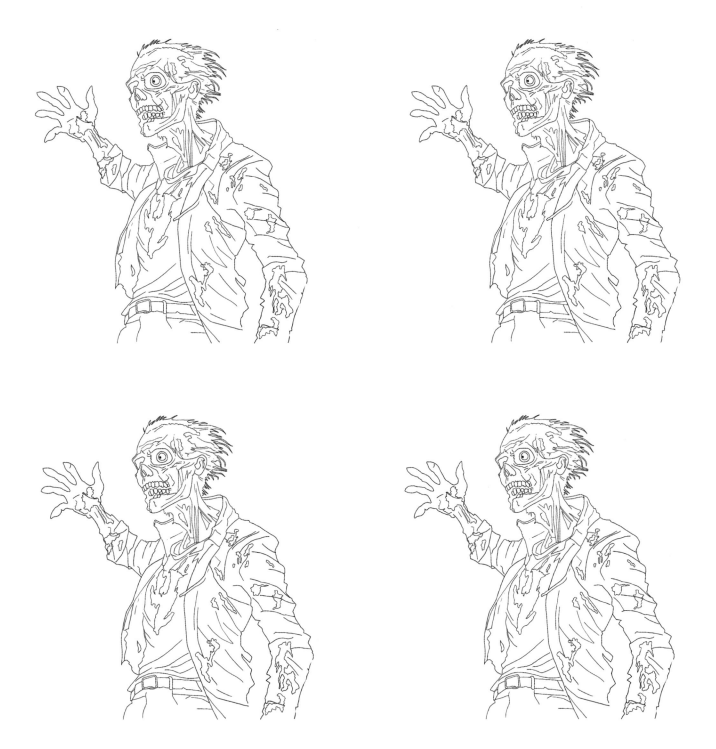

Practice Pages

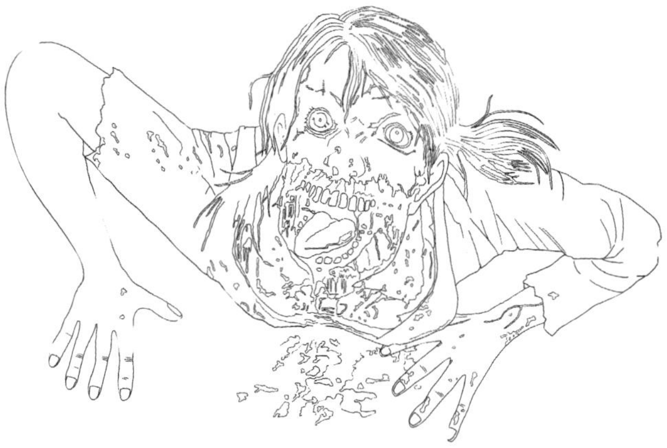

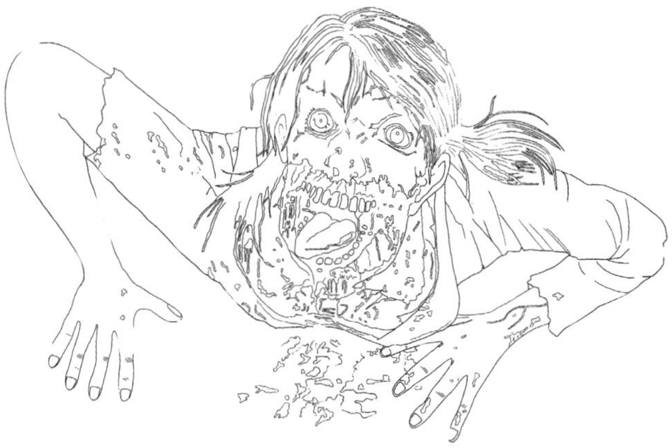

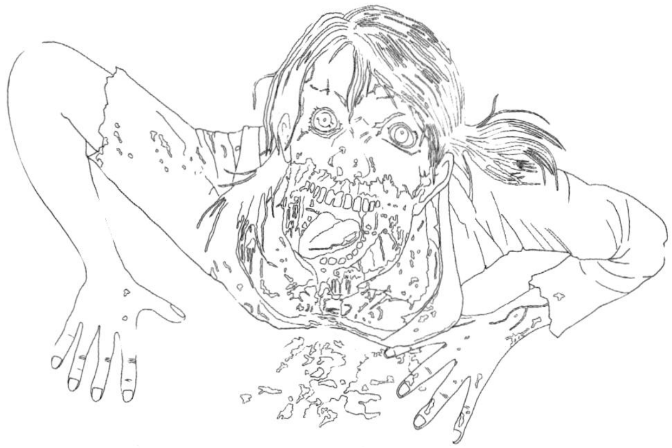

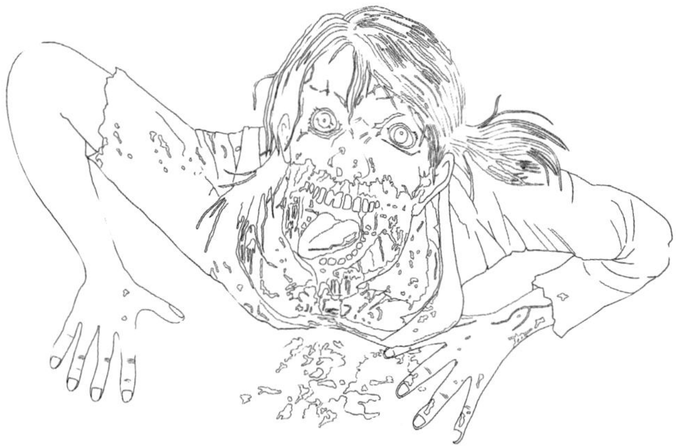

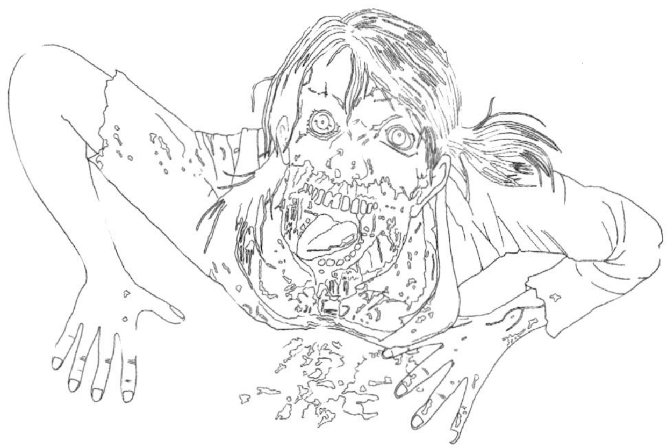

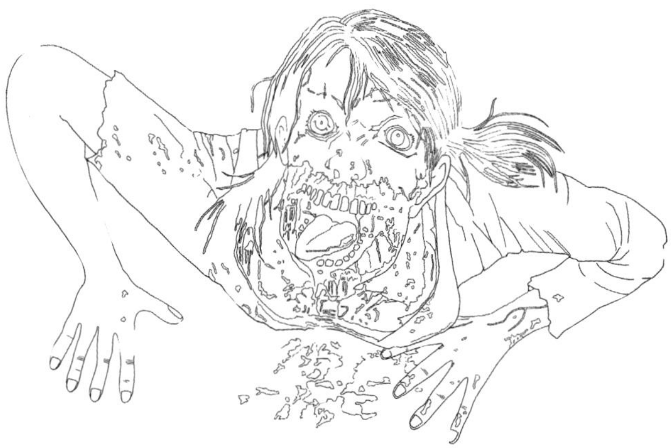

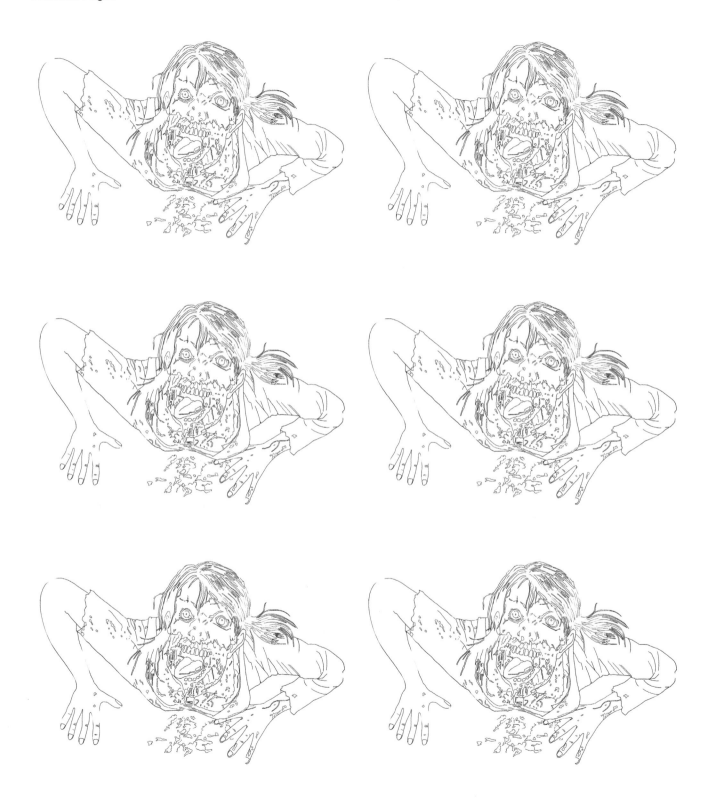

Practice Pages

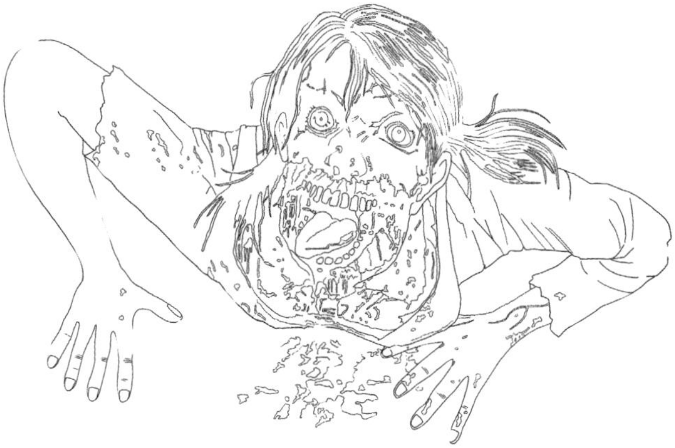

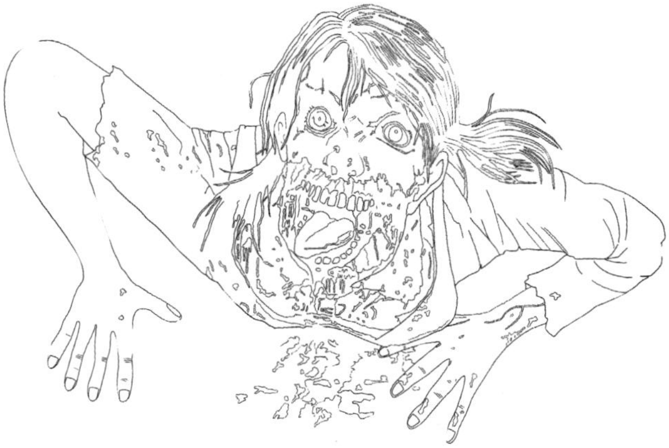

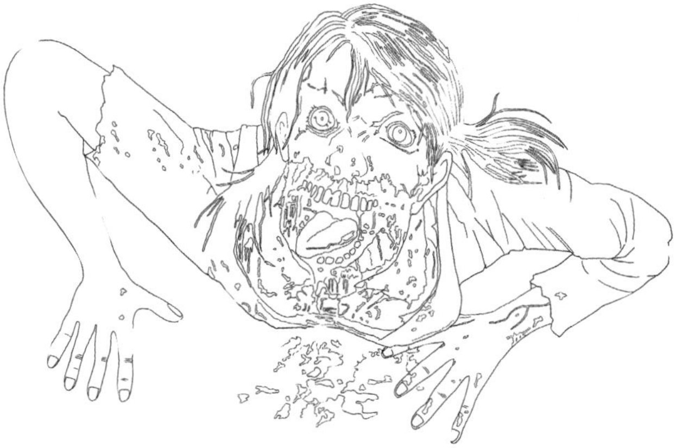

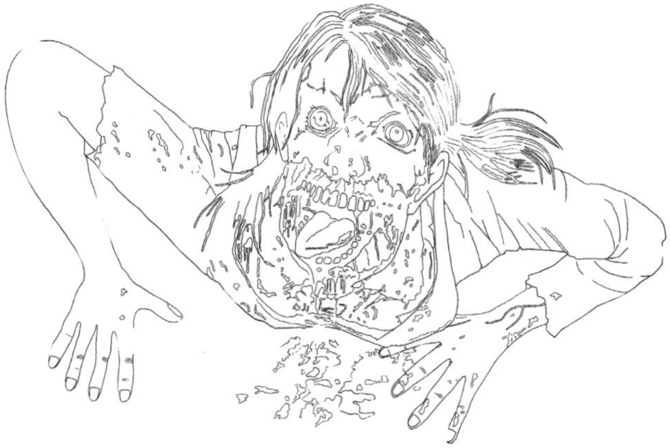

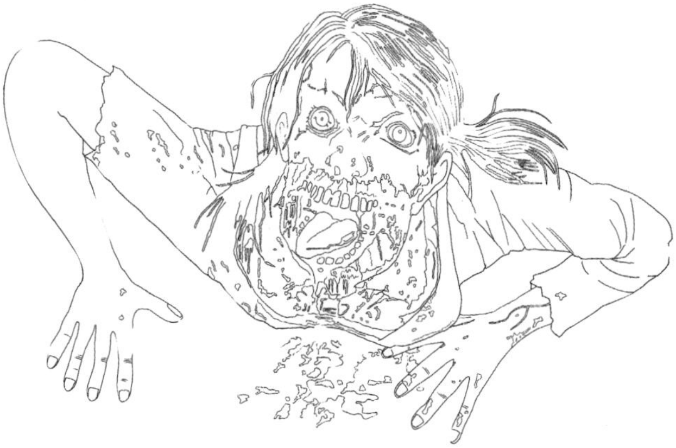

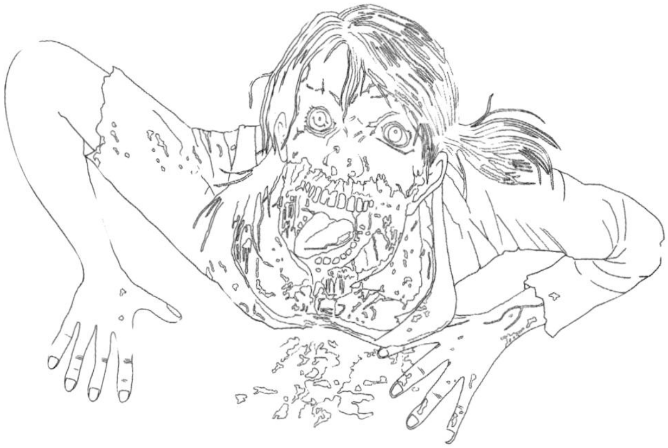

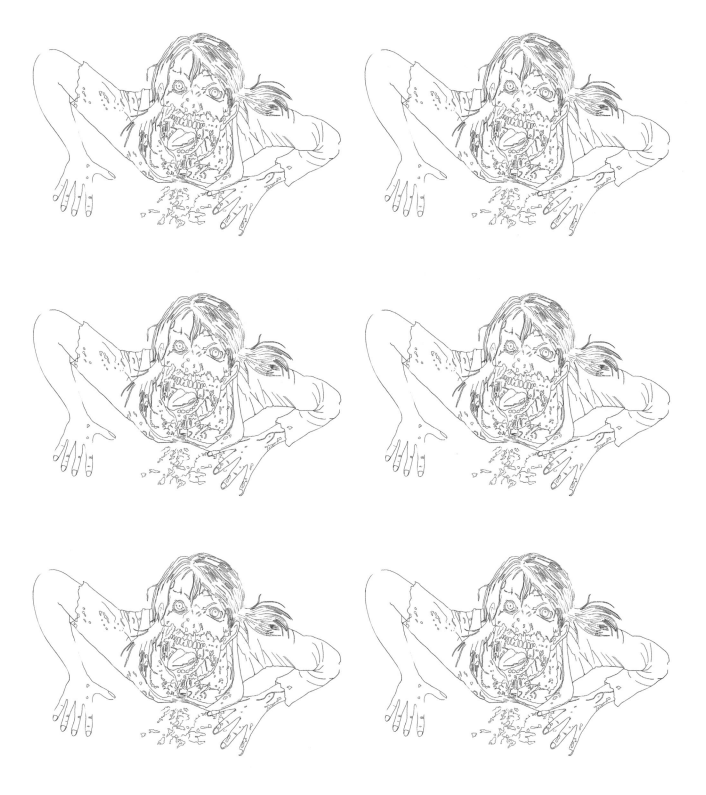

Practice Pages

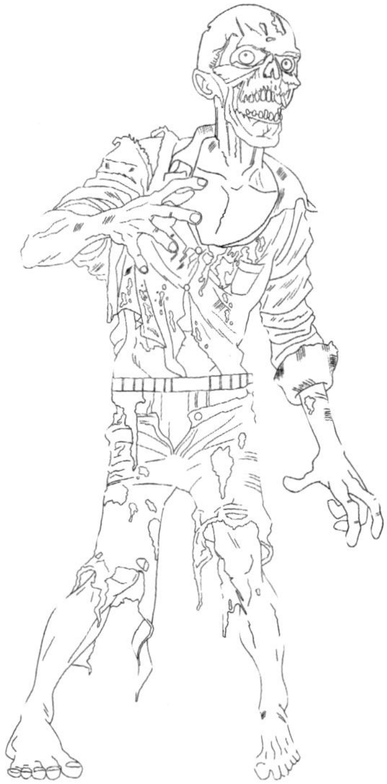
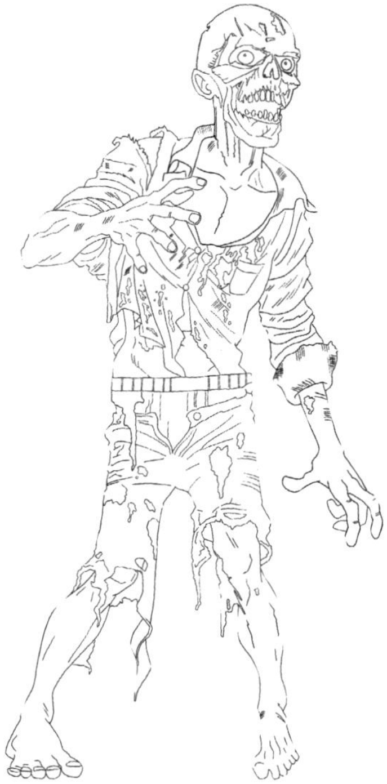
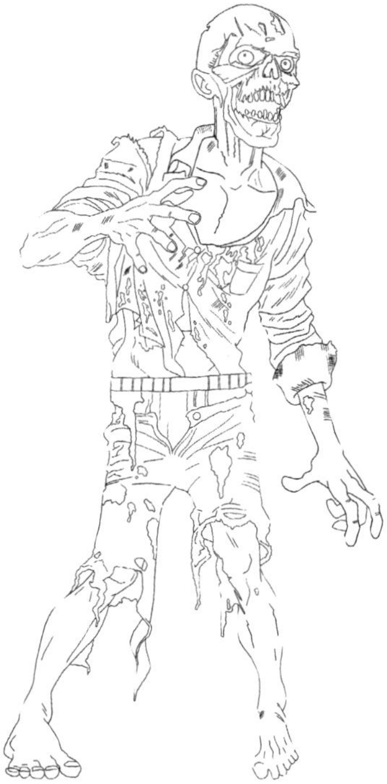
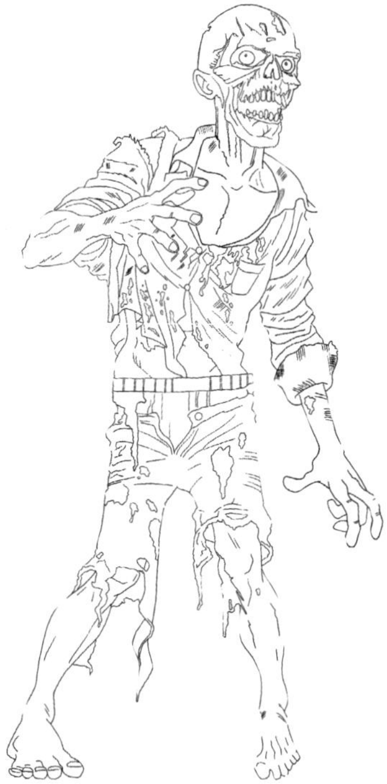
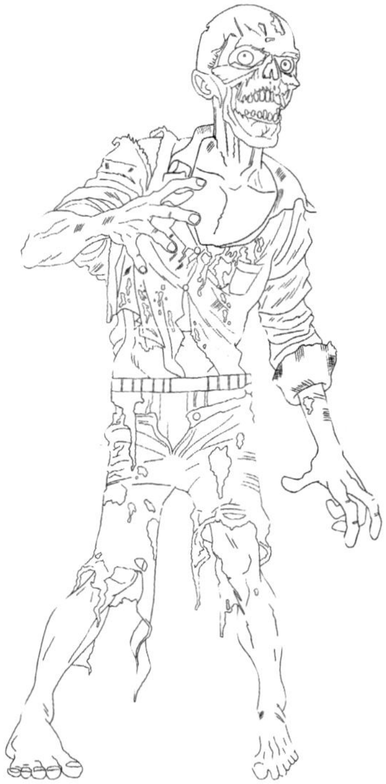
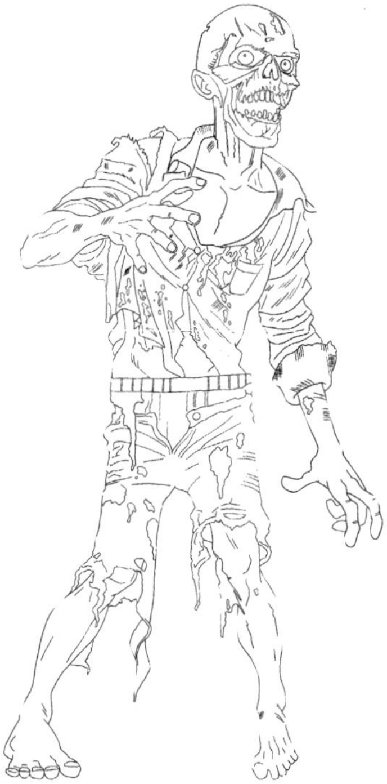

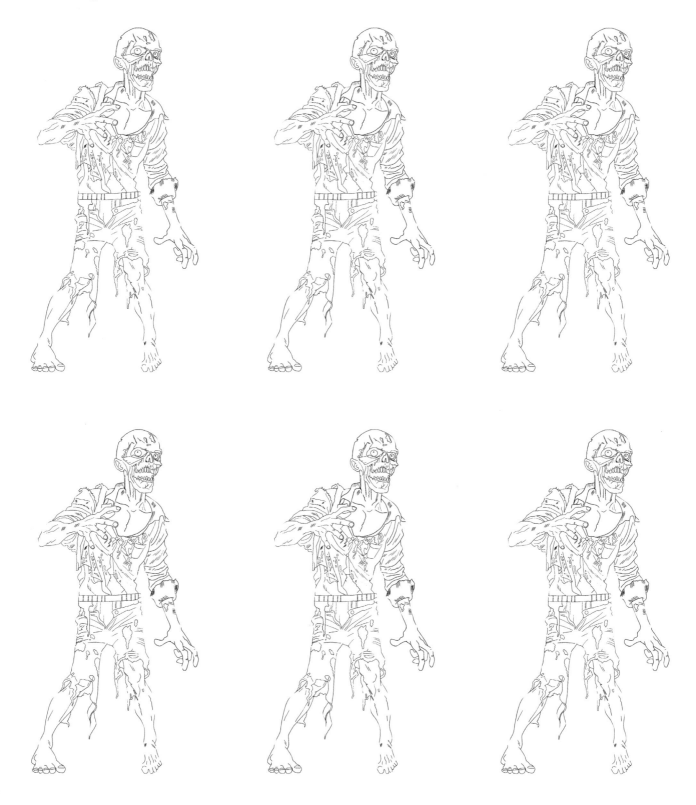

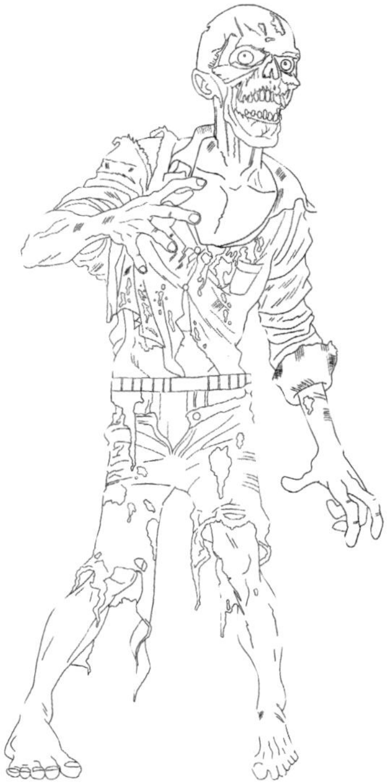

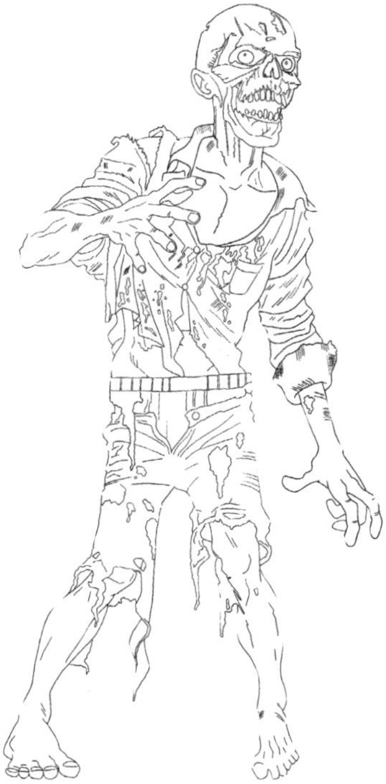

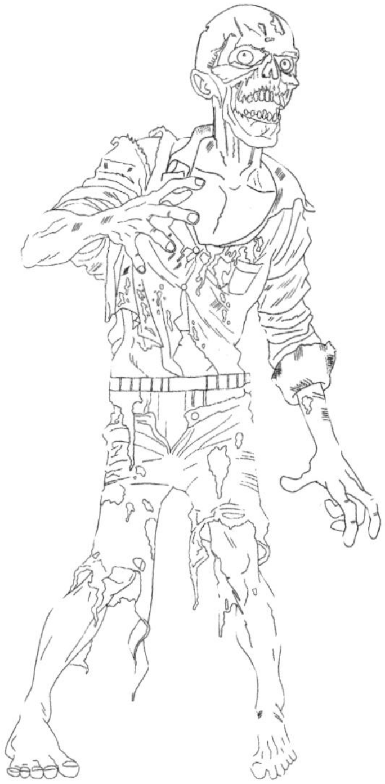

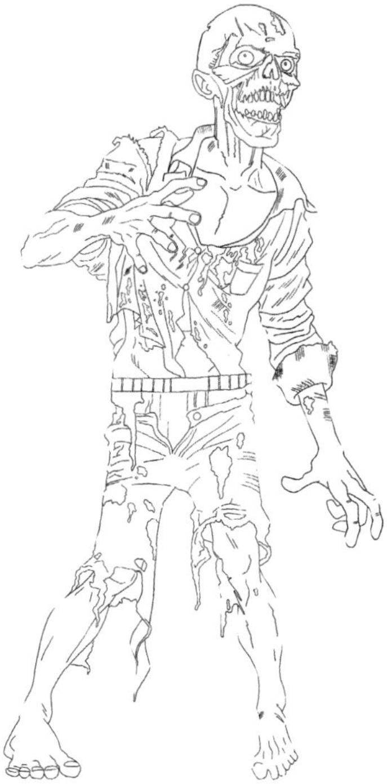

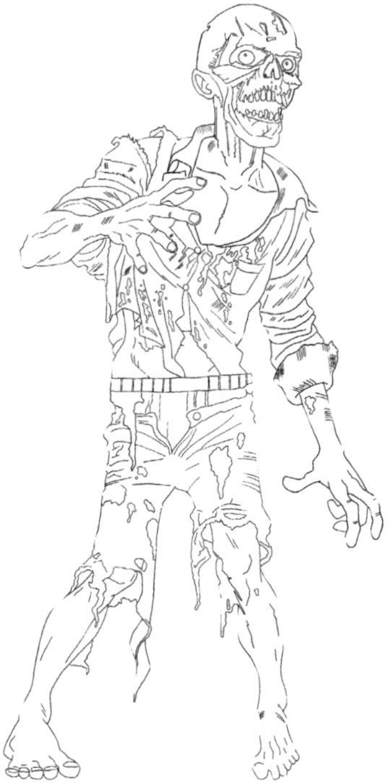

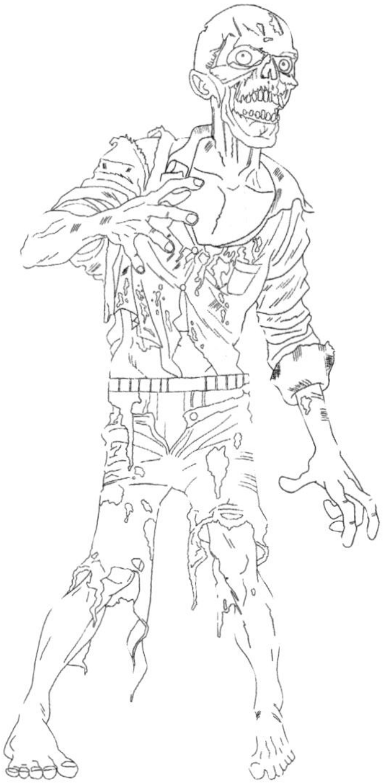

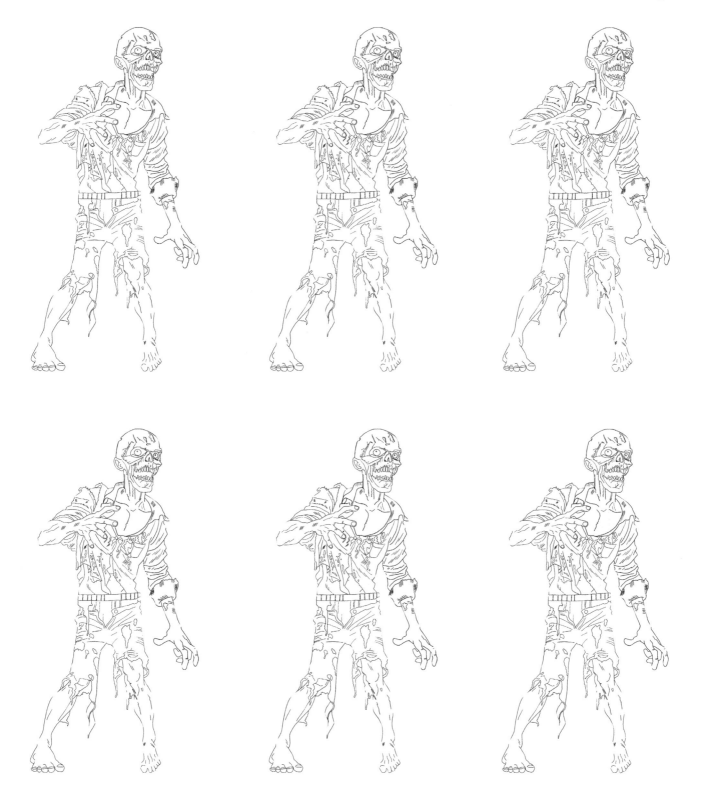

Practice Pages

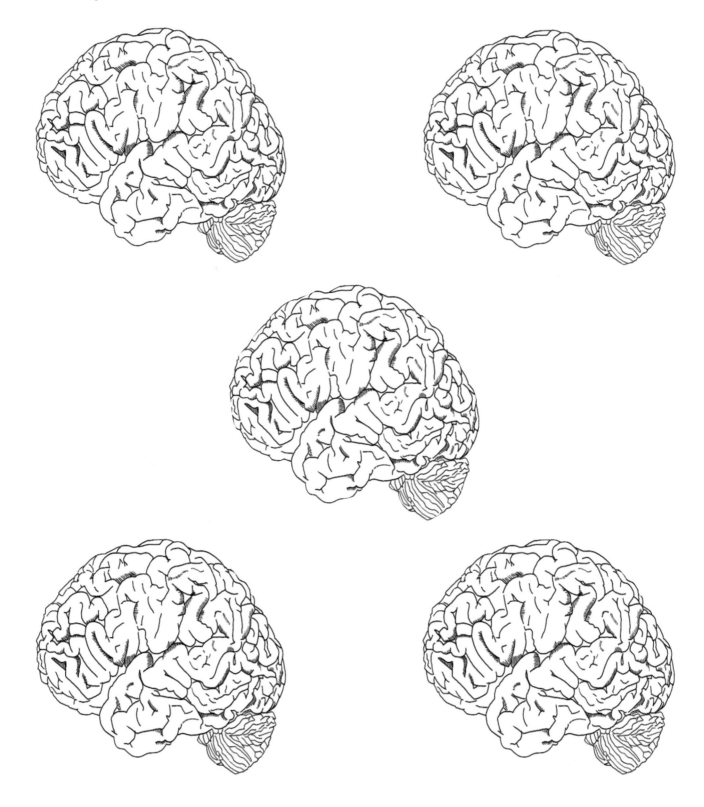

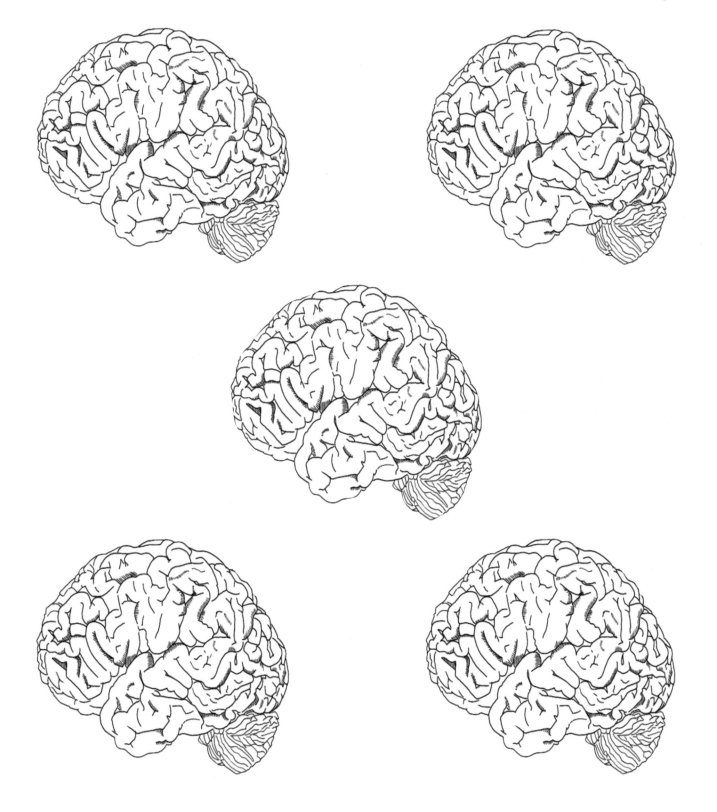

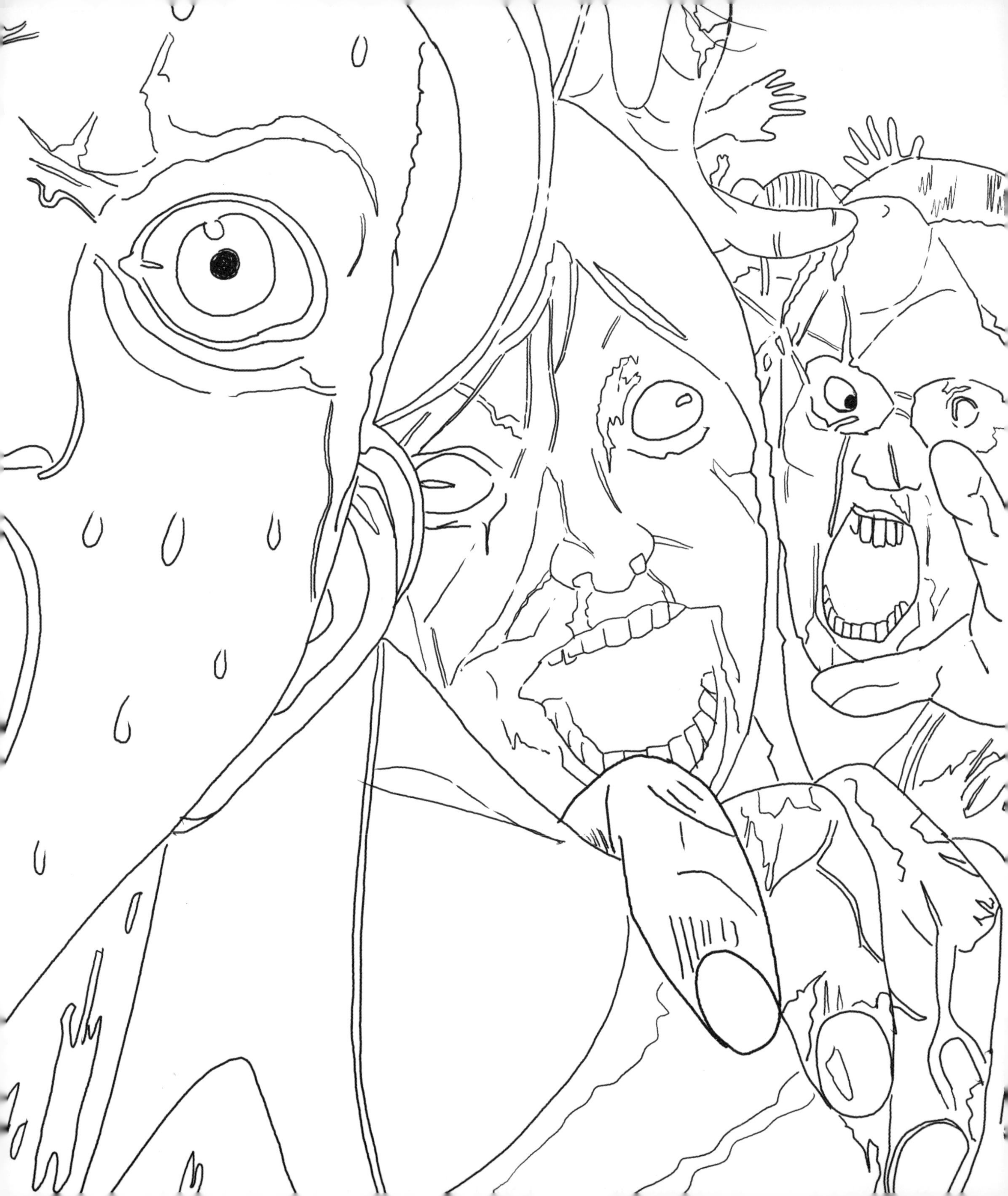

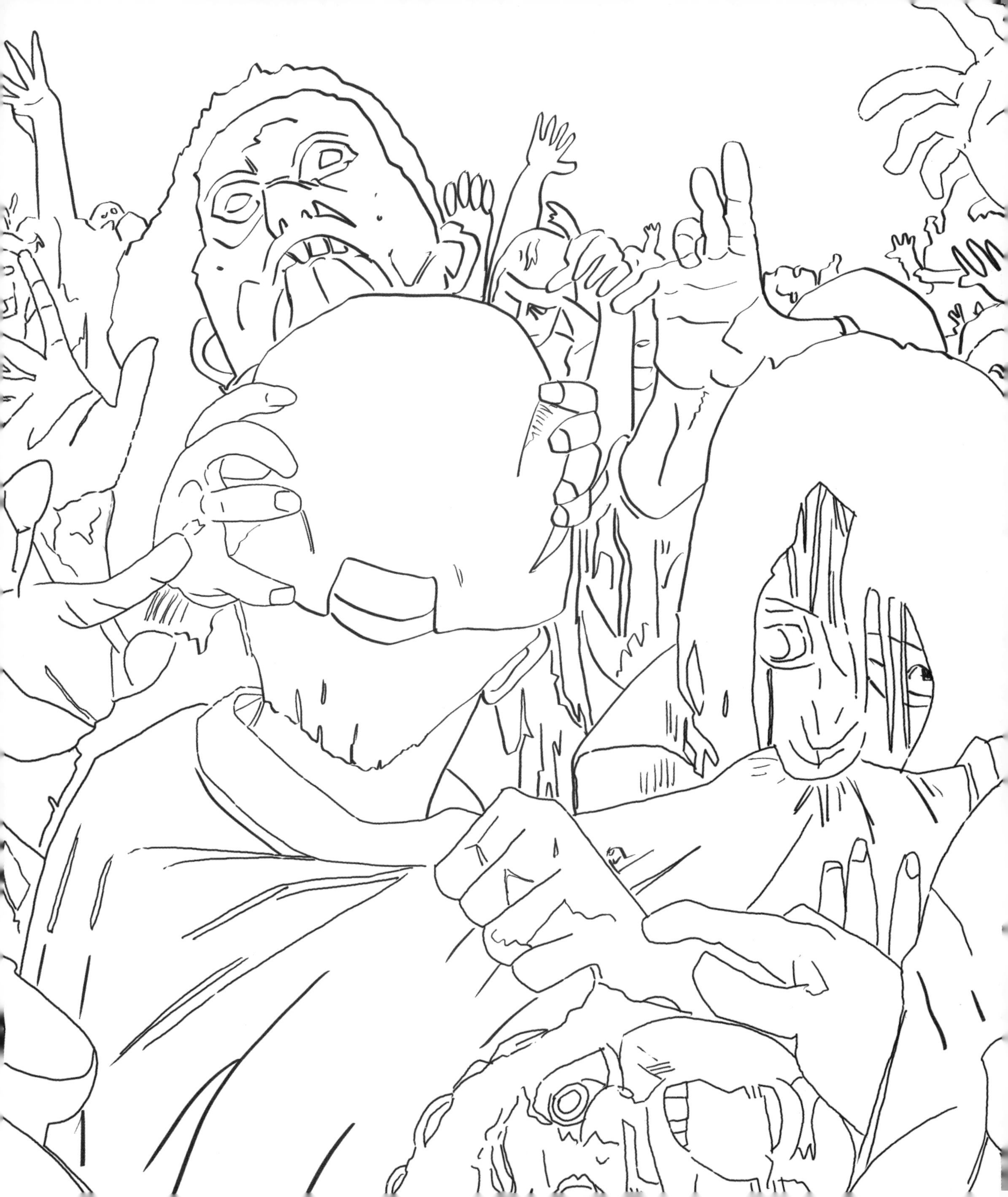

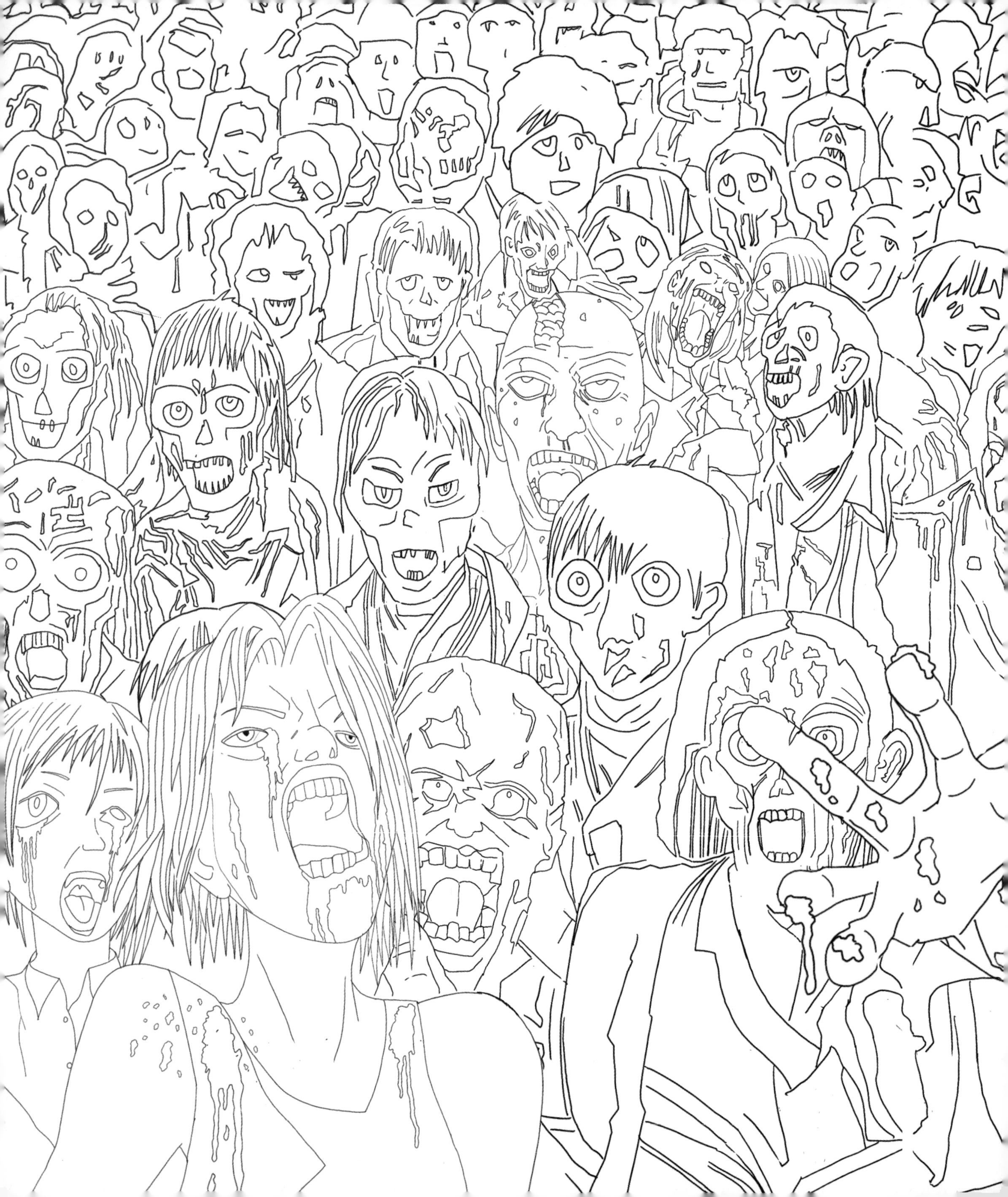

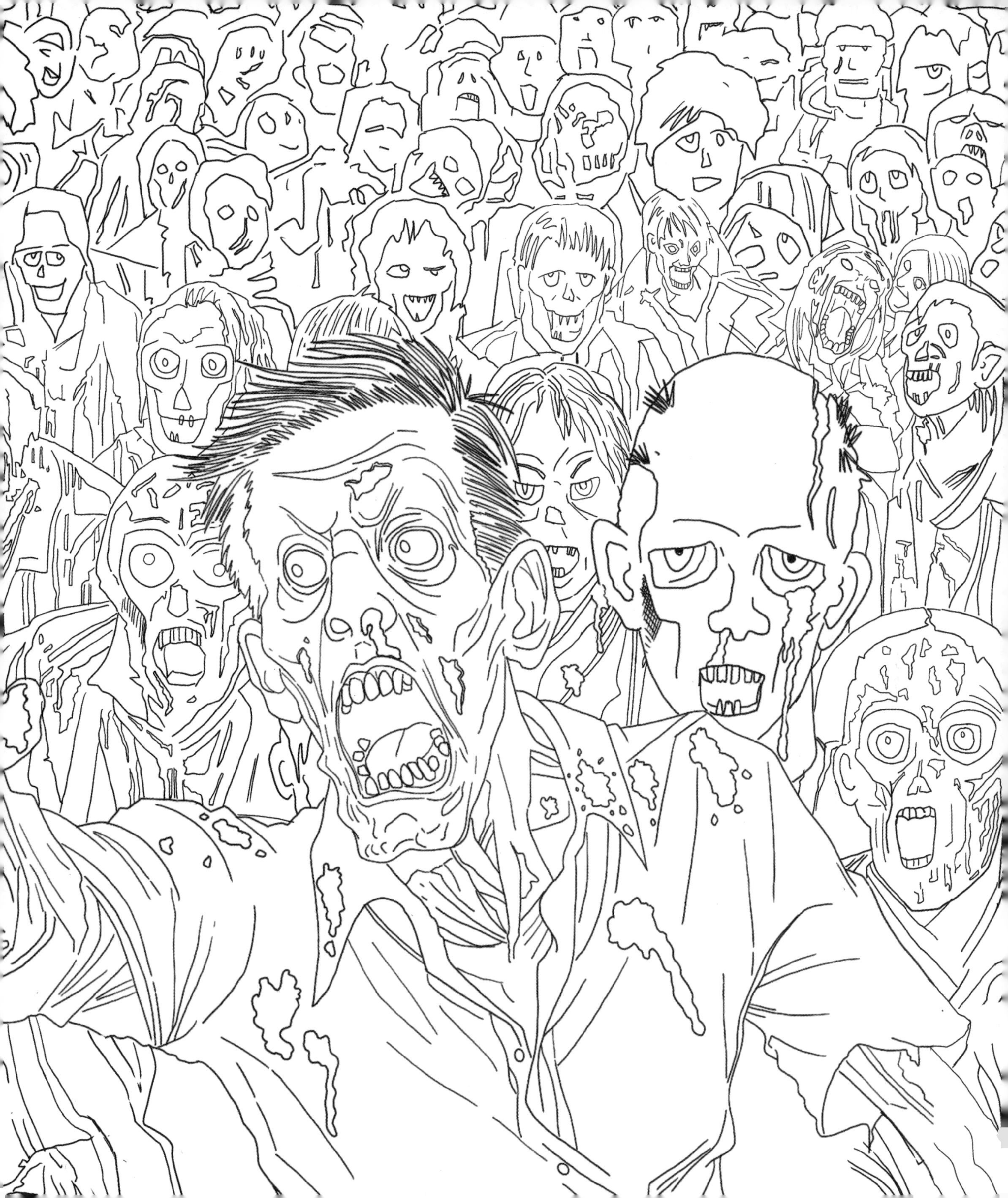

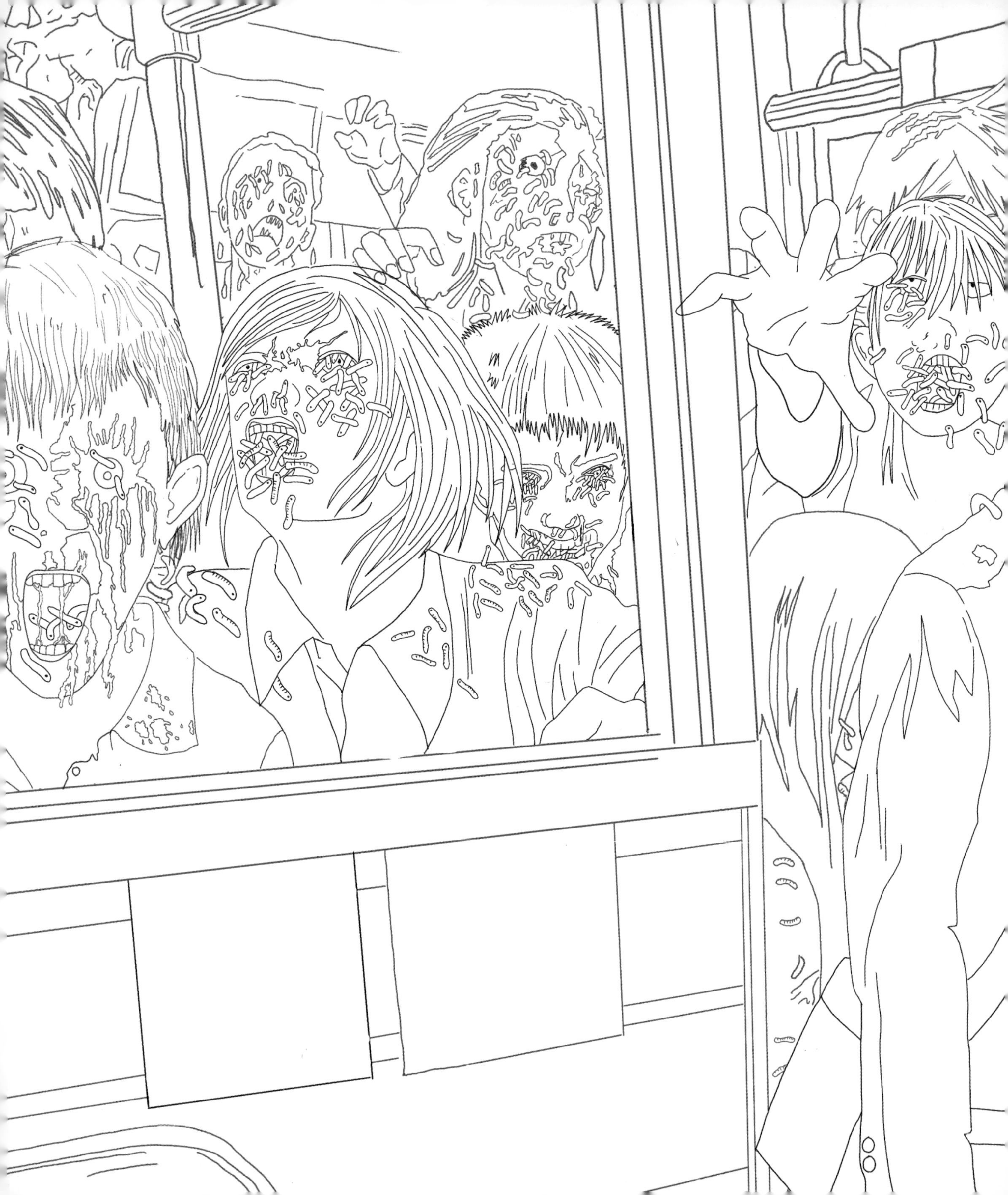

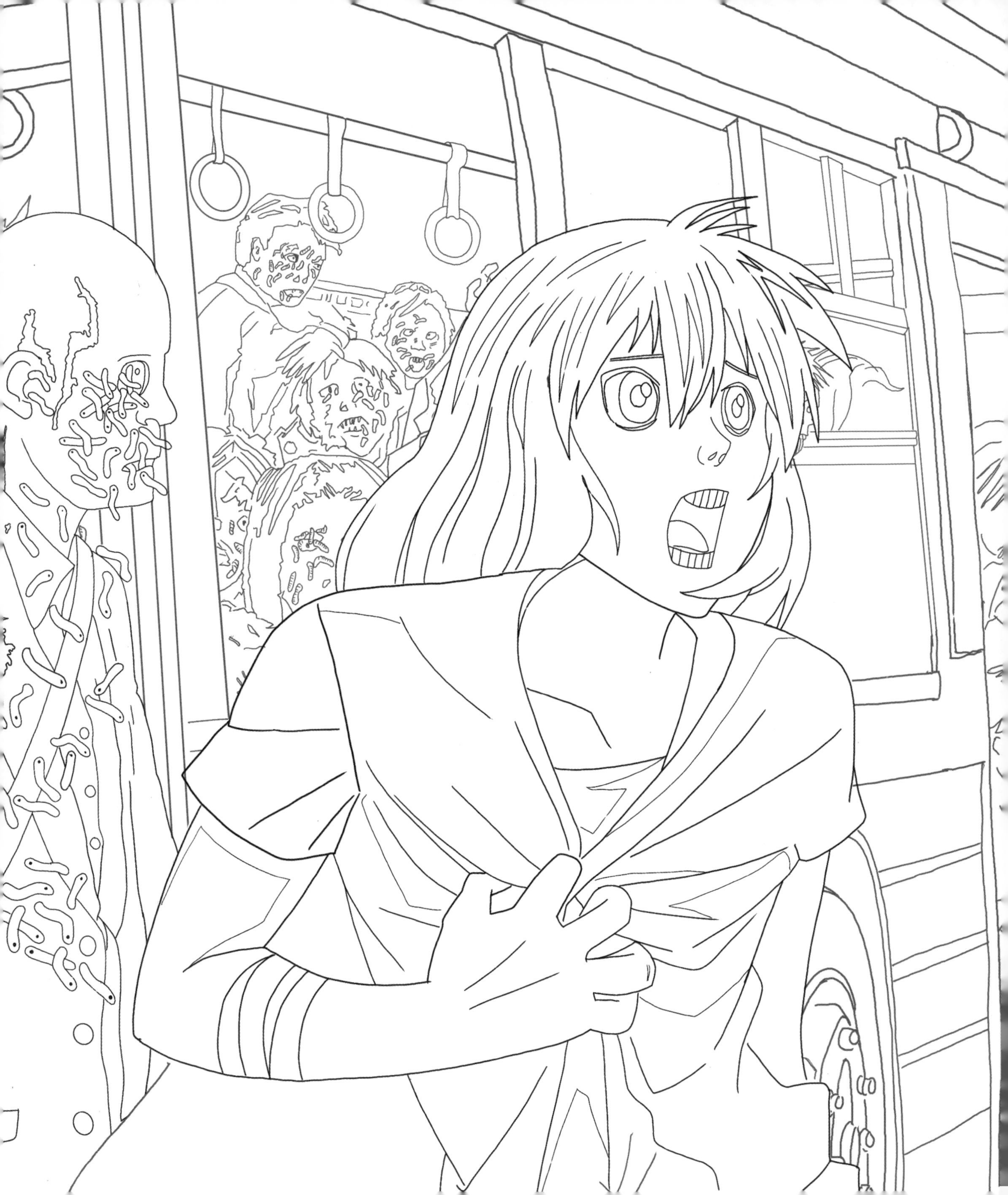

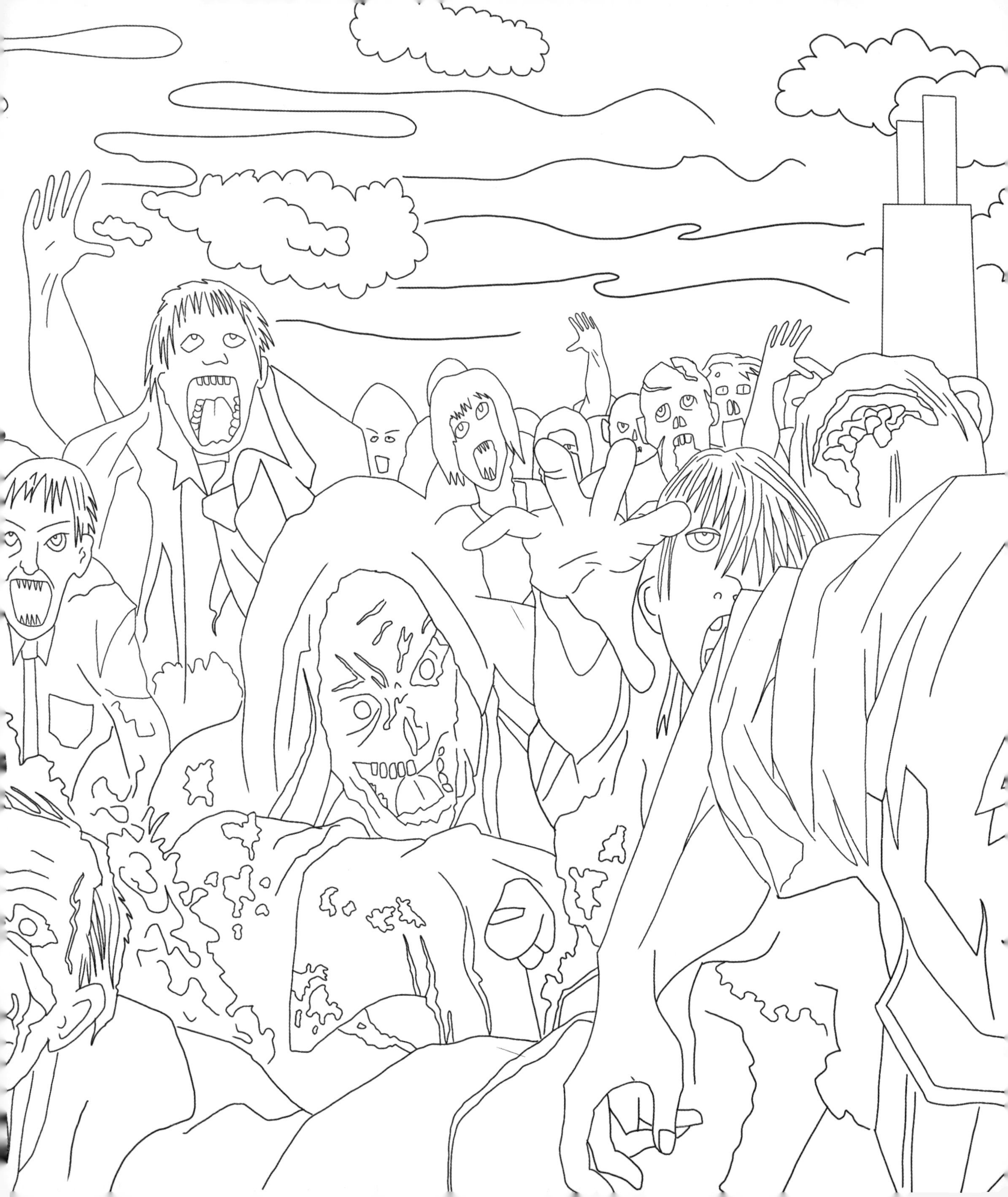

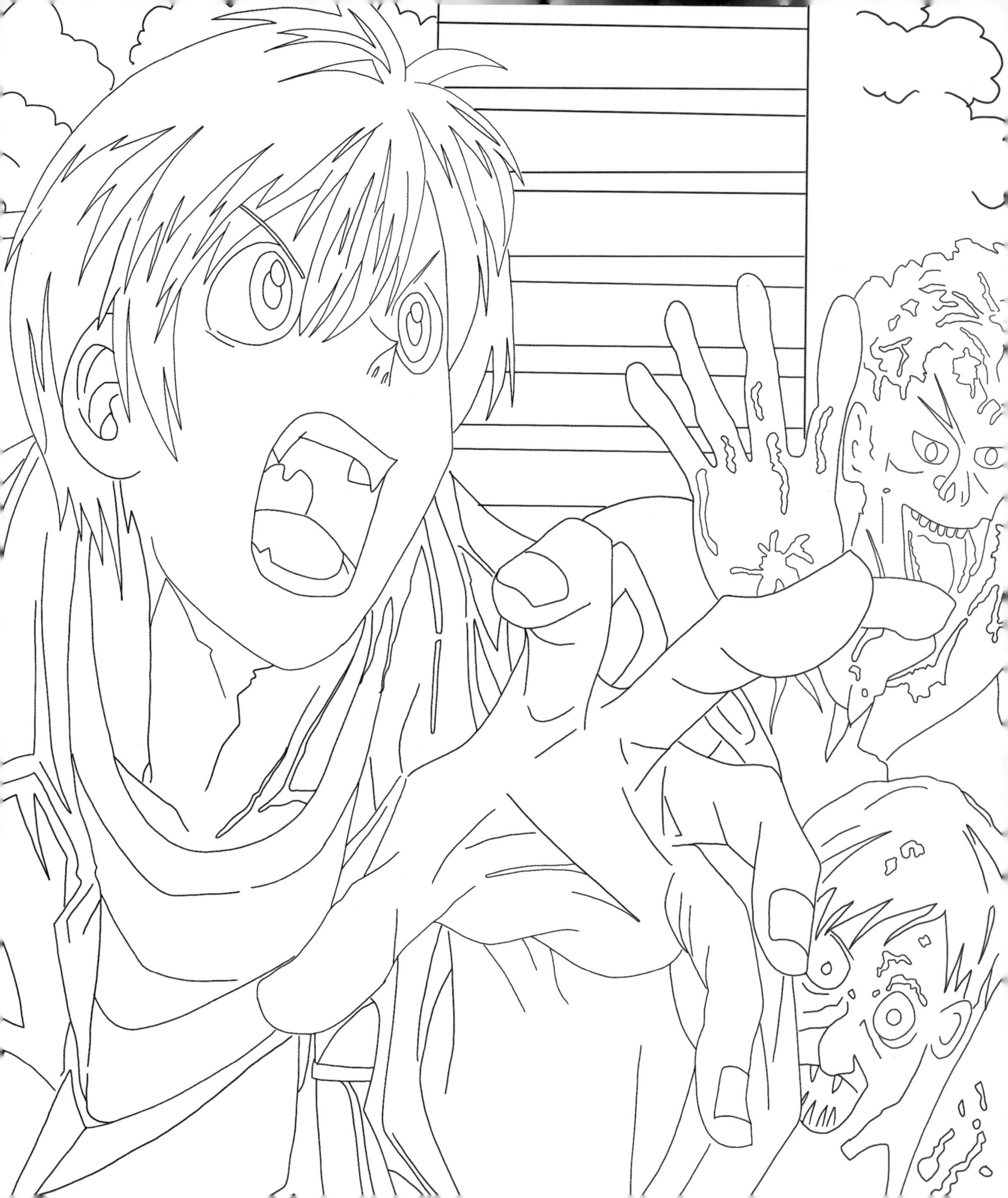

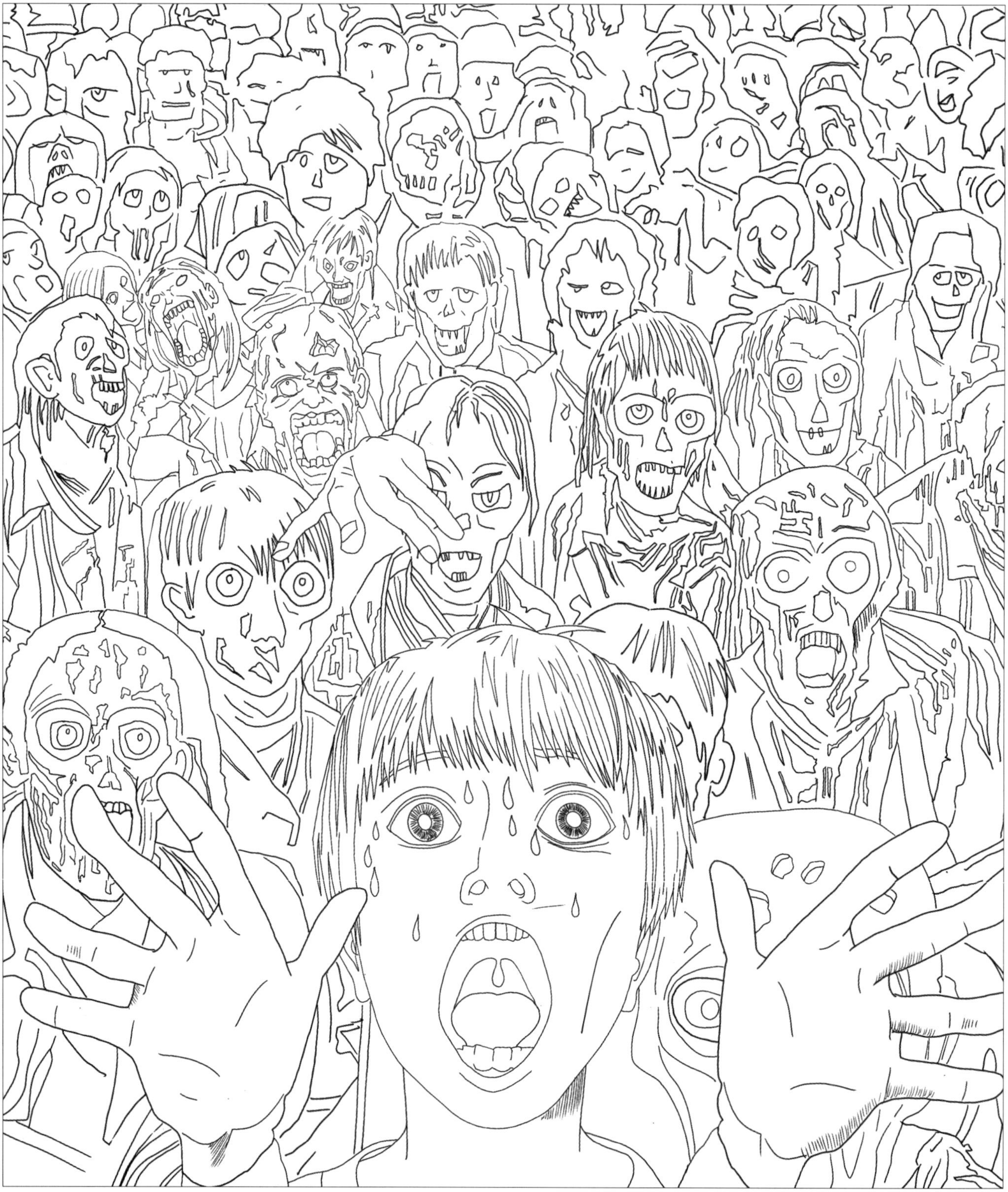

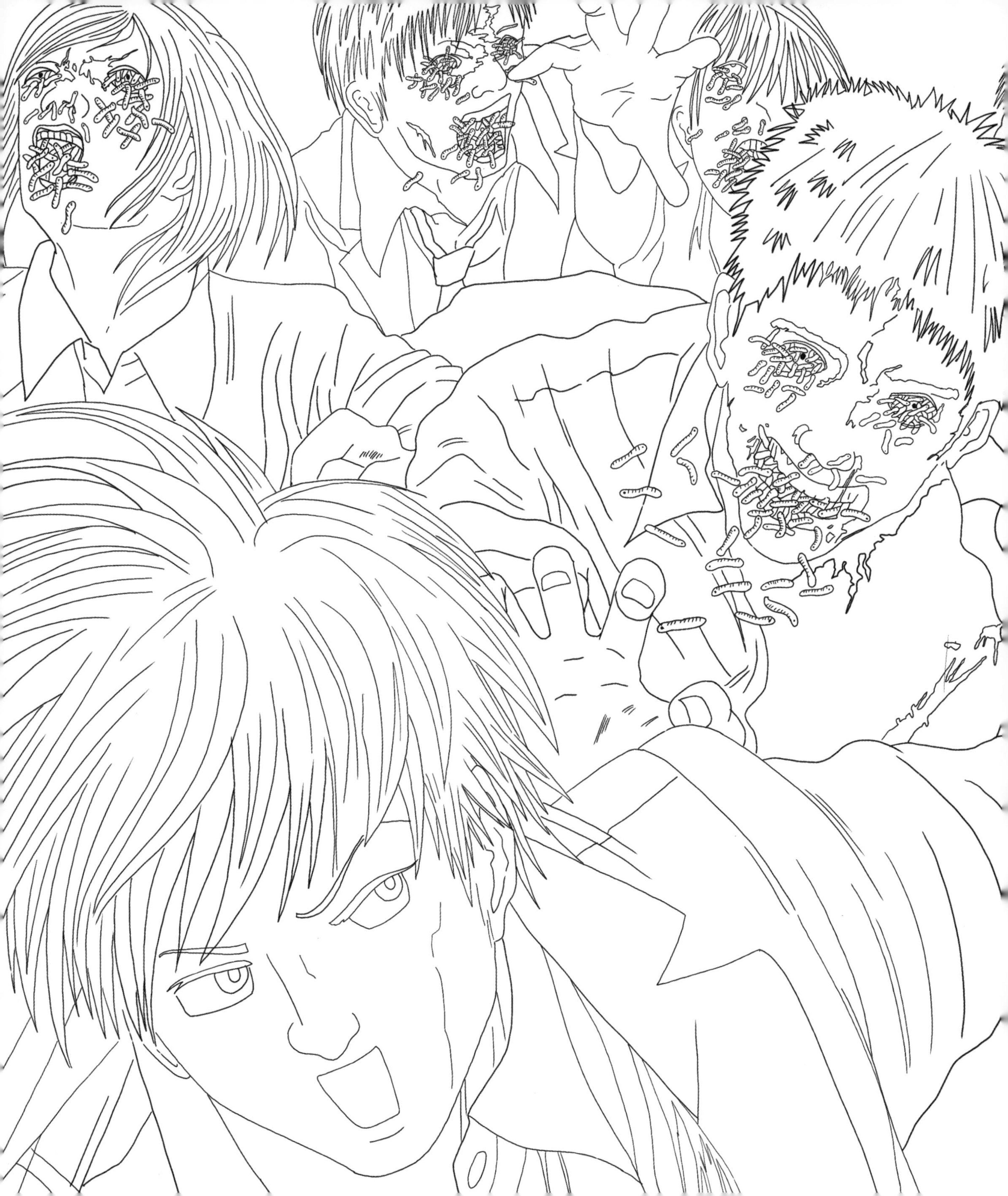

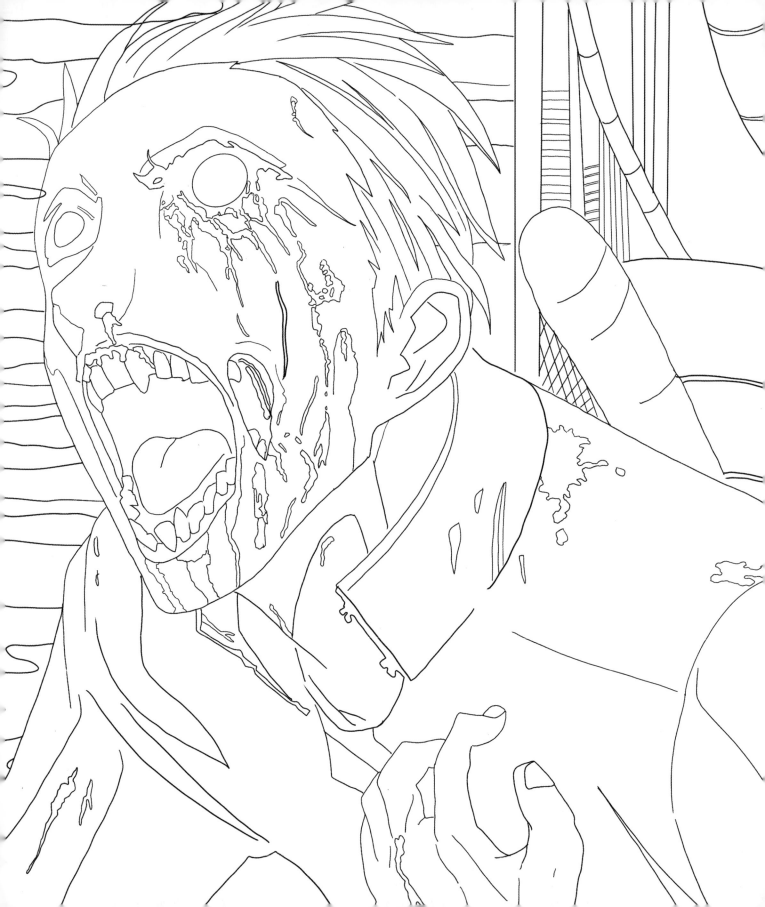

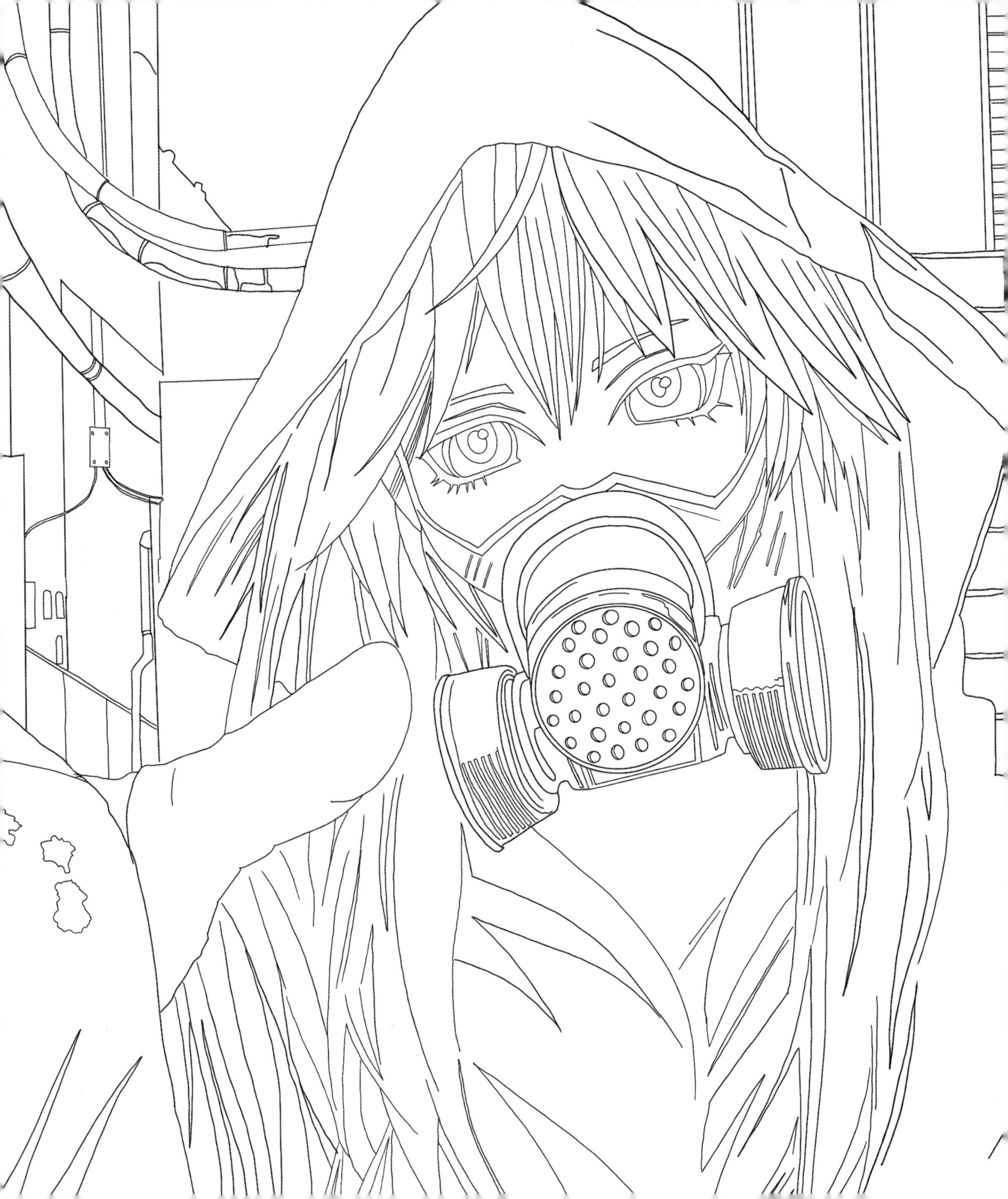

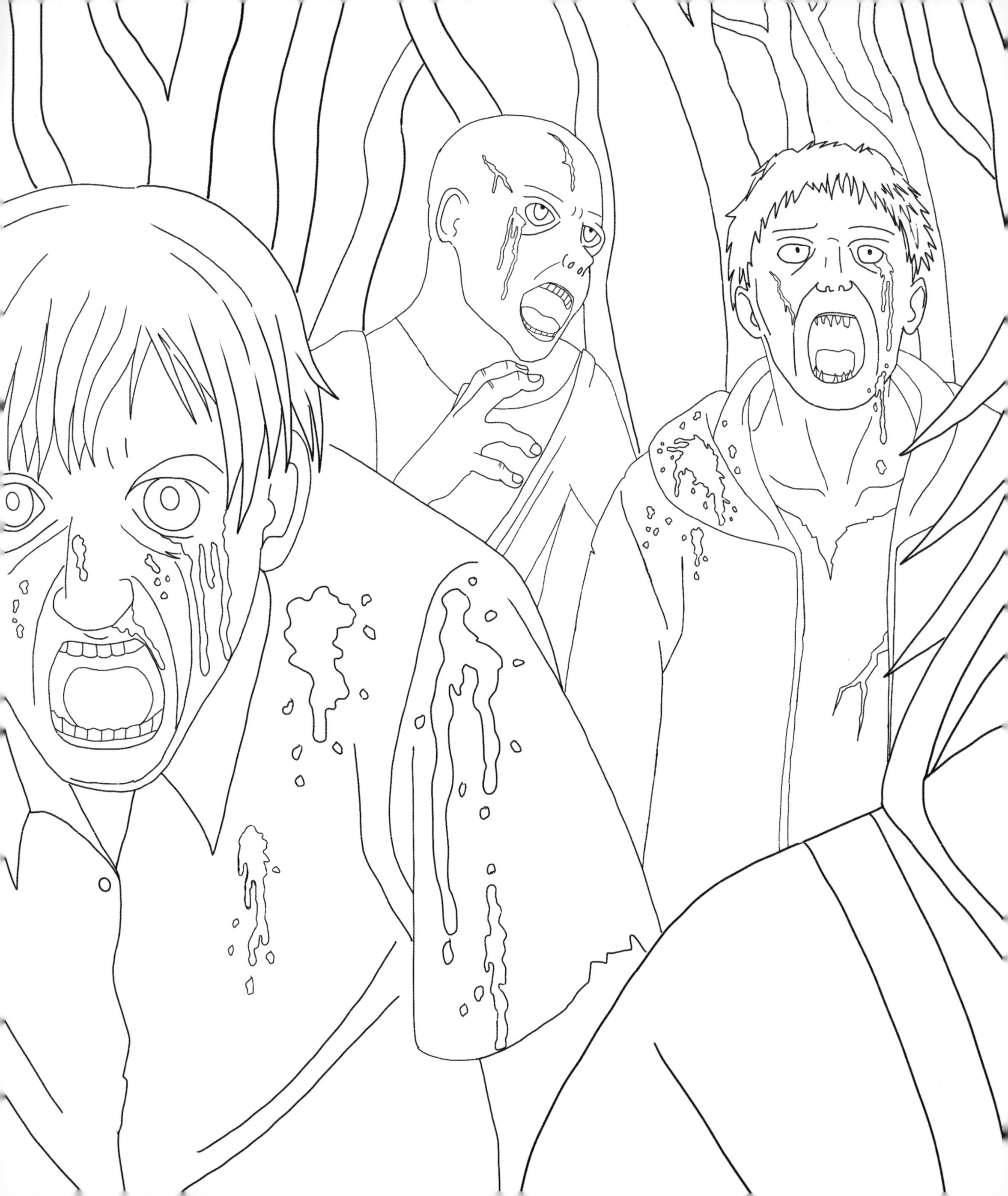

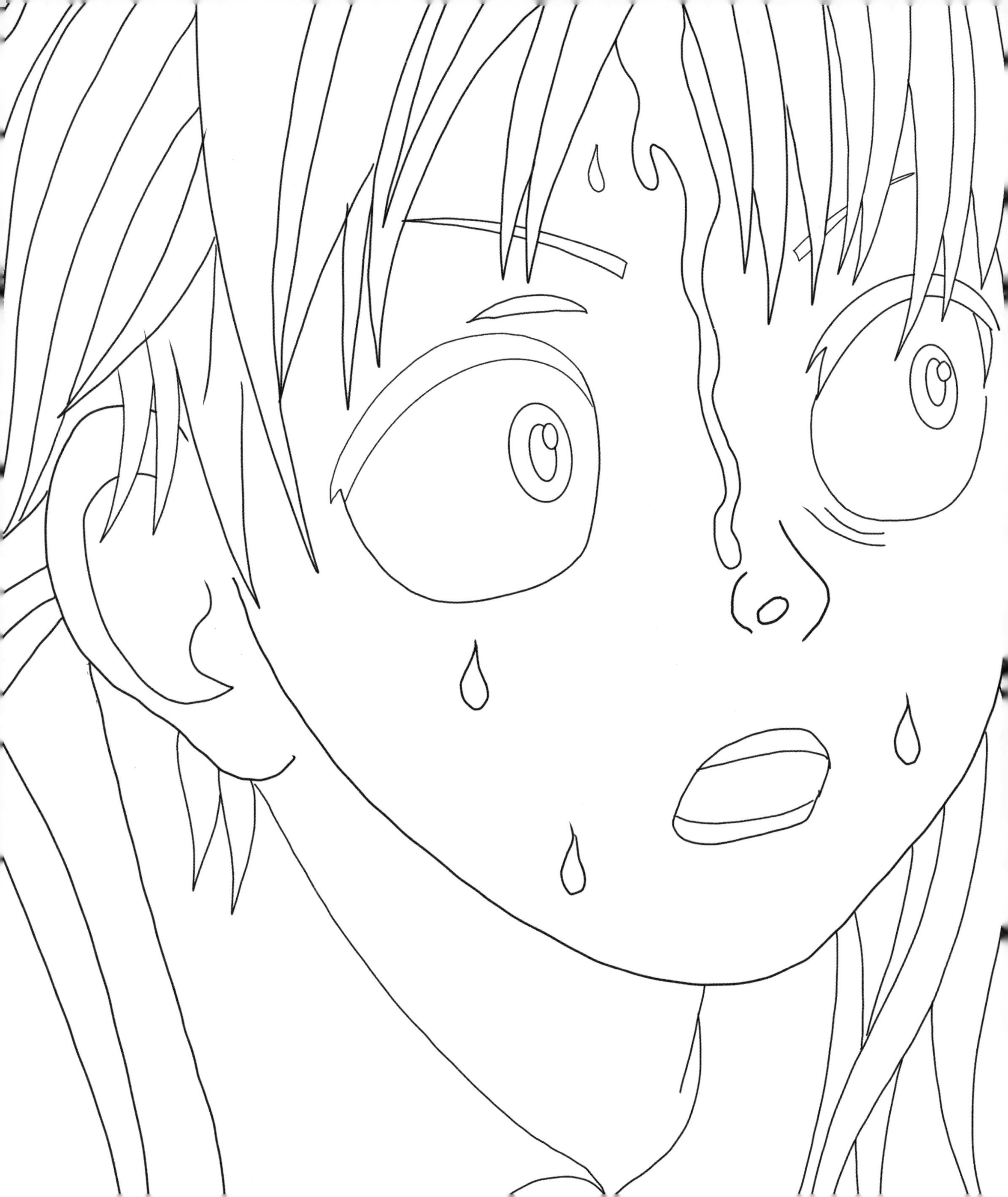

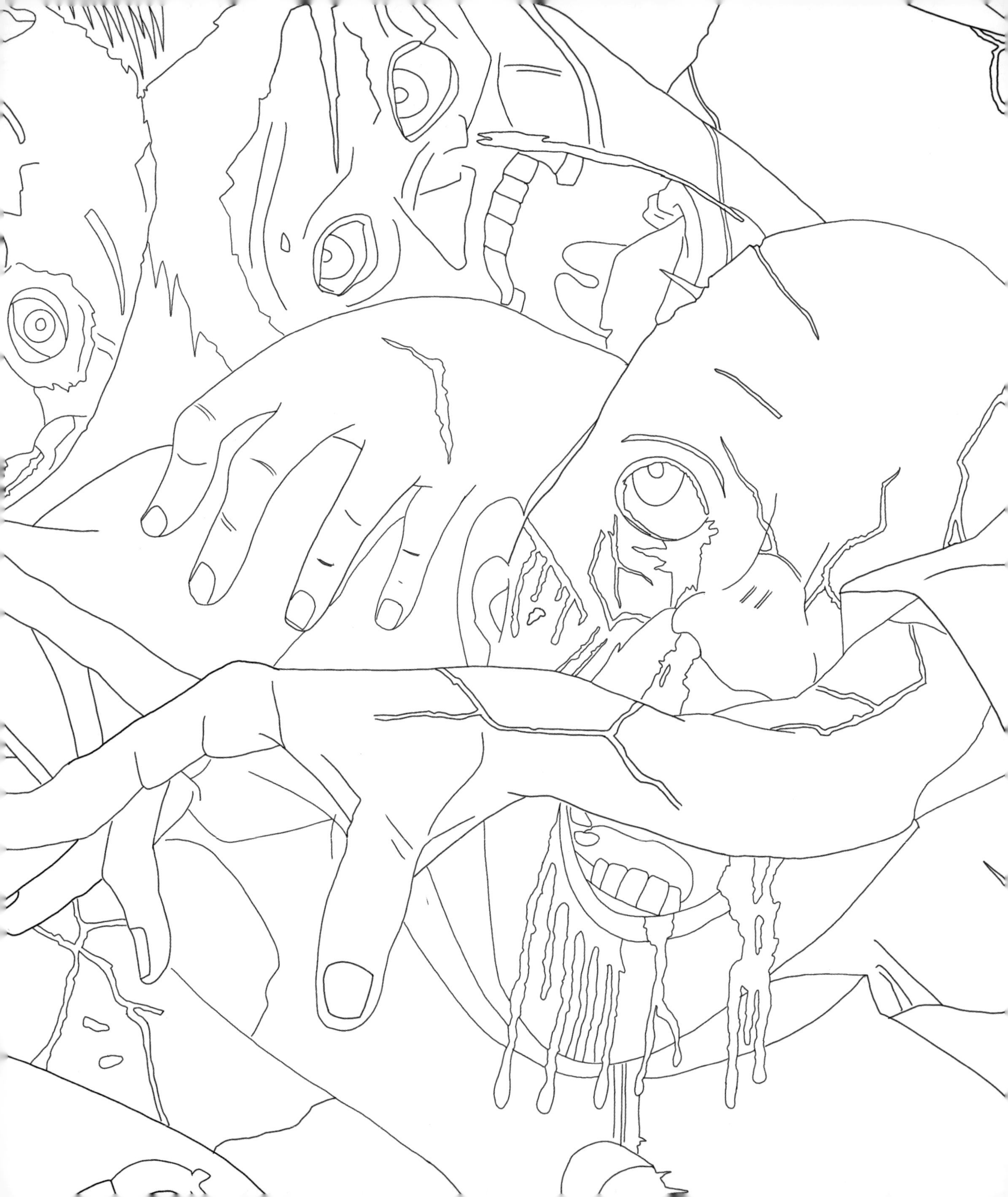

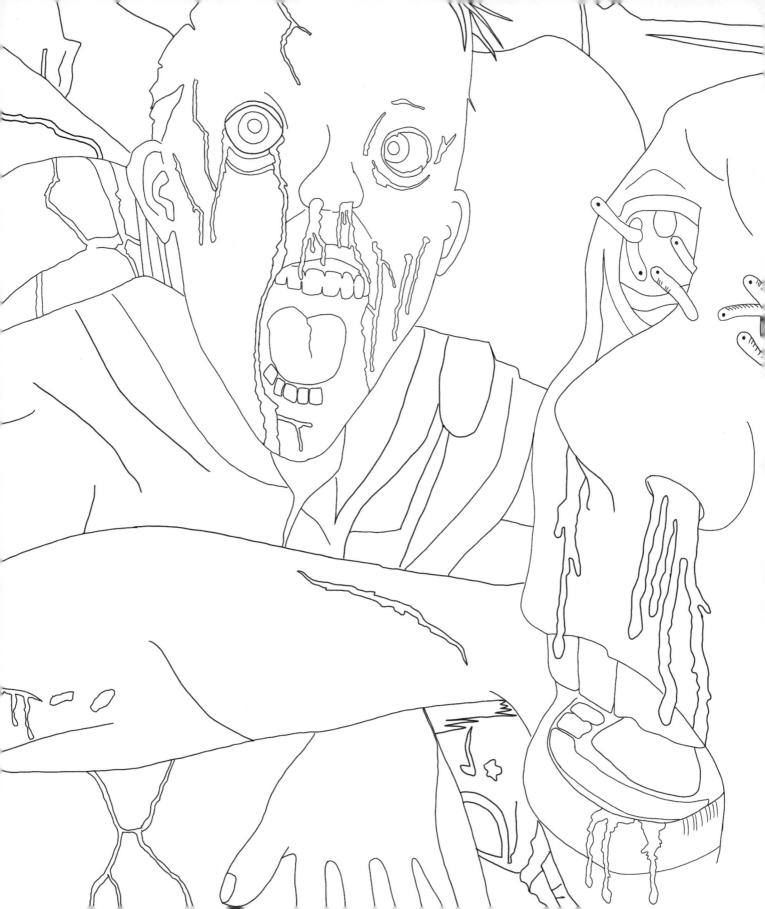

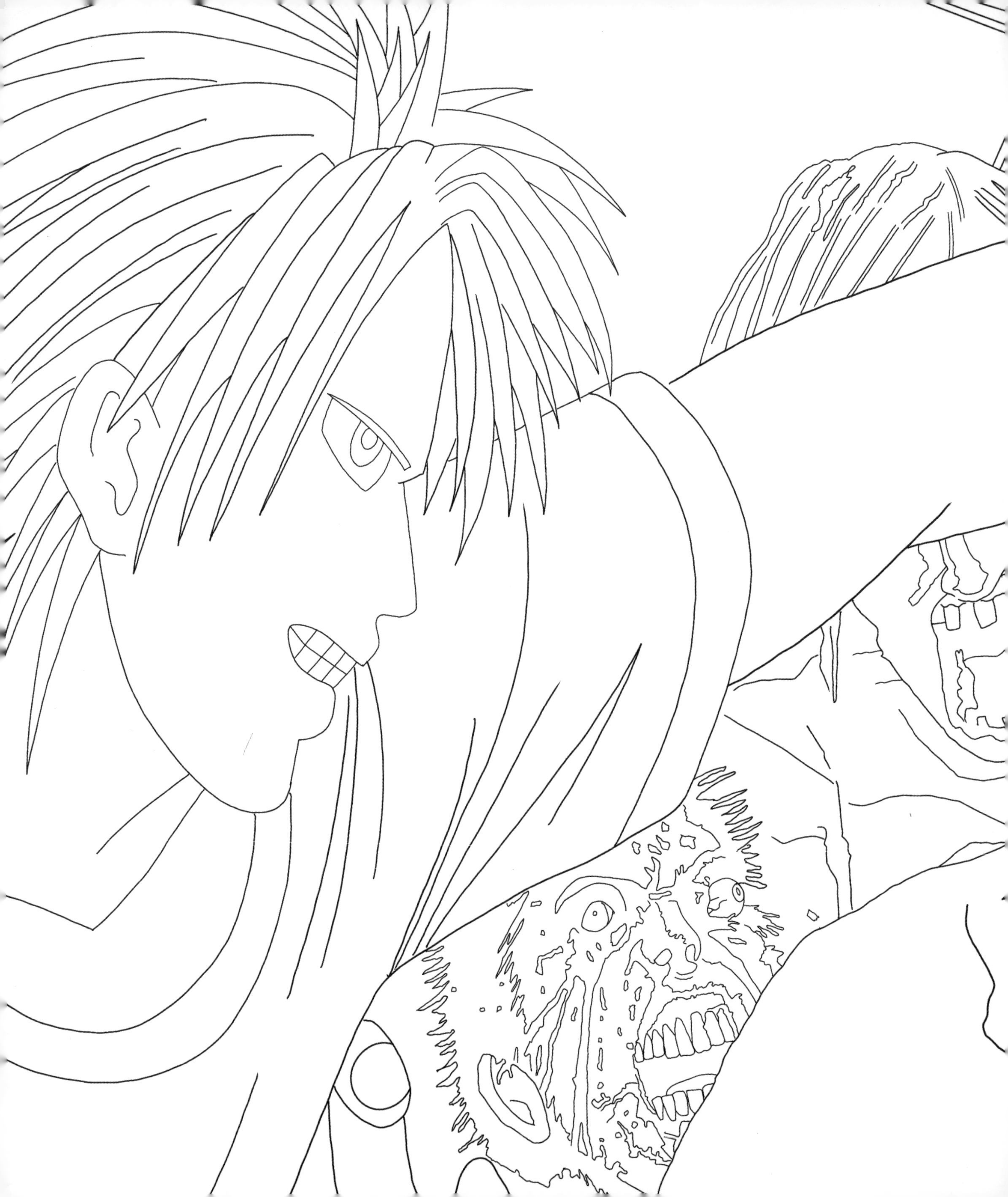

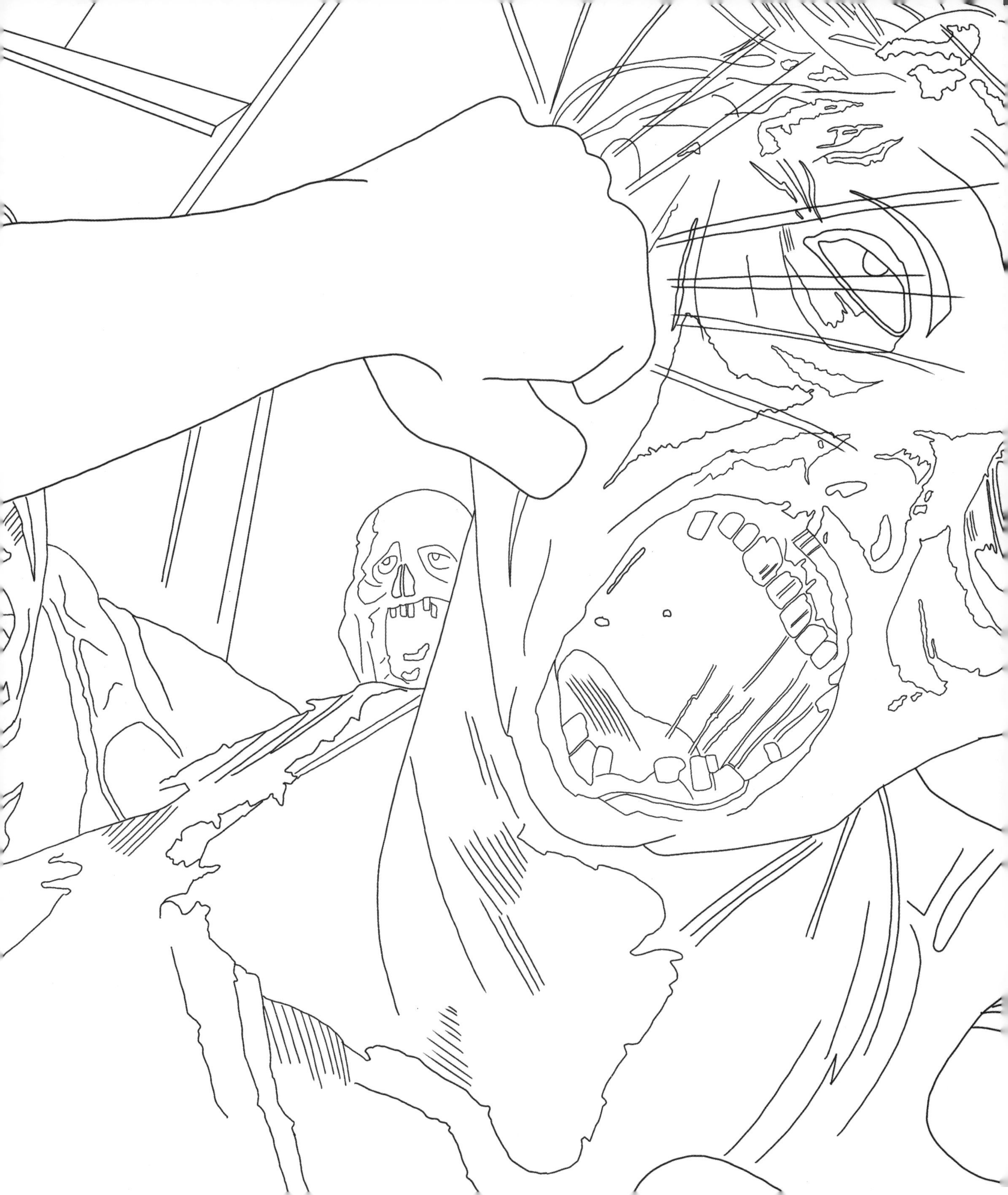

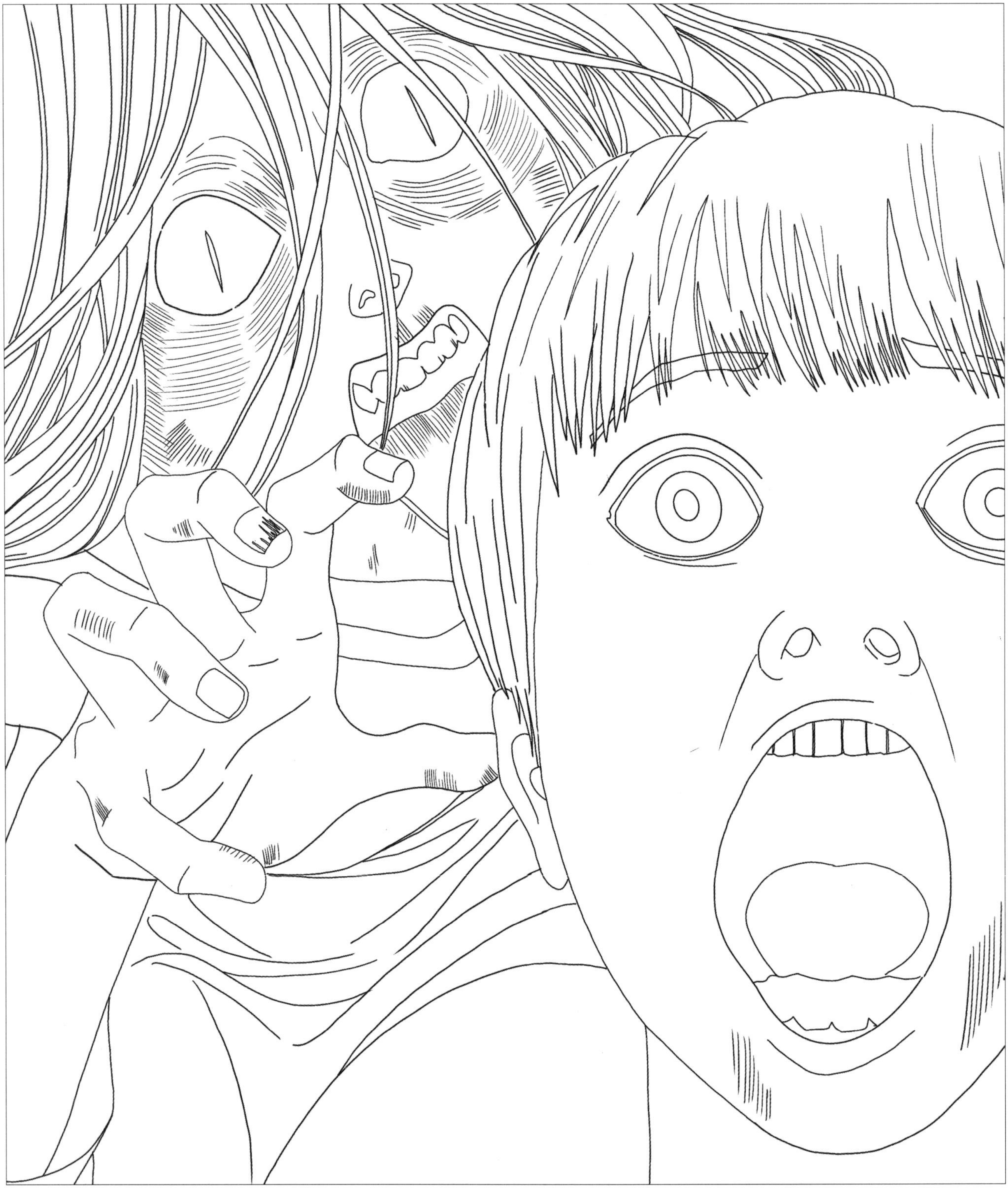

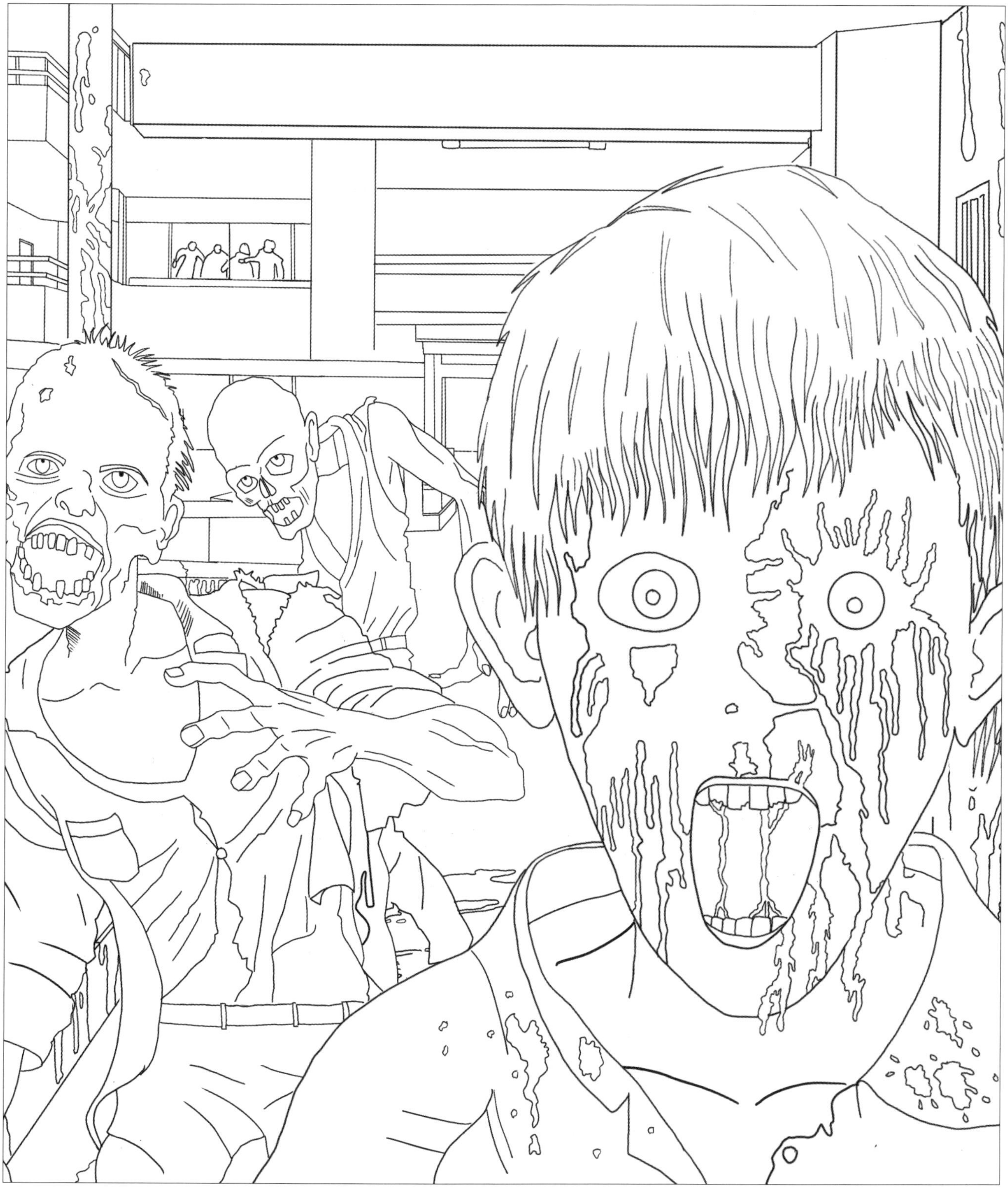

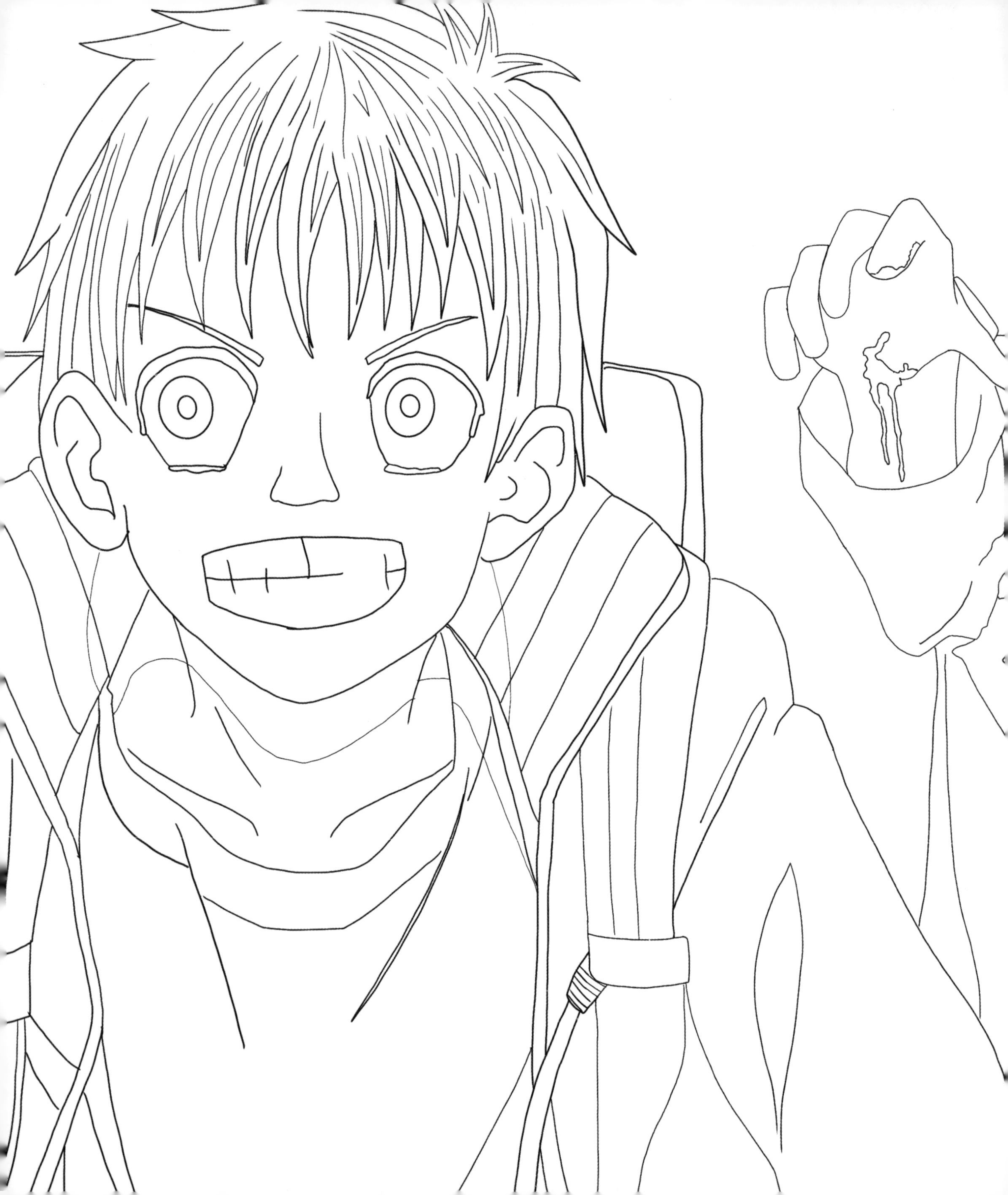

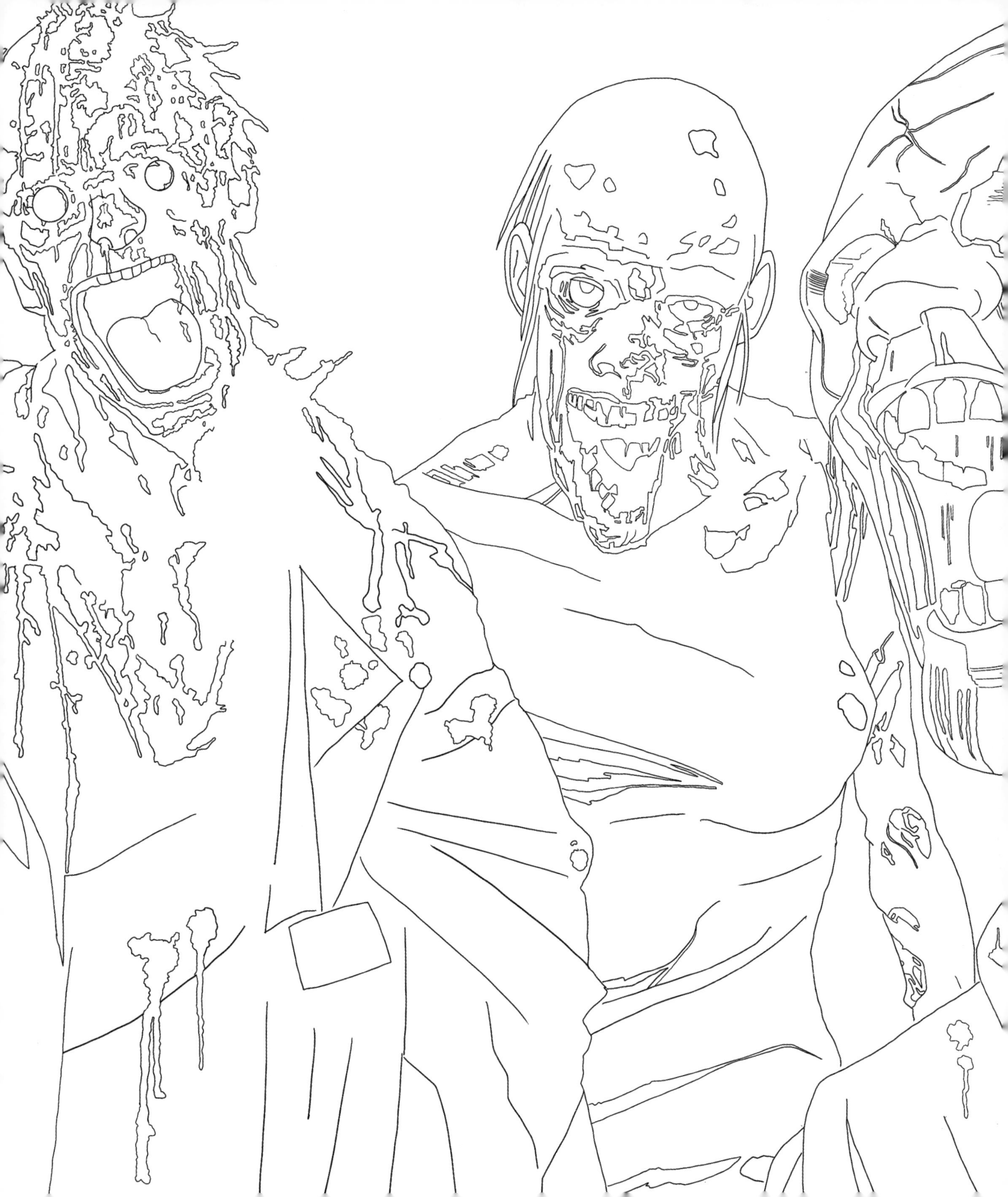

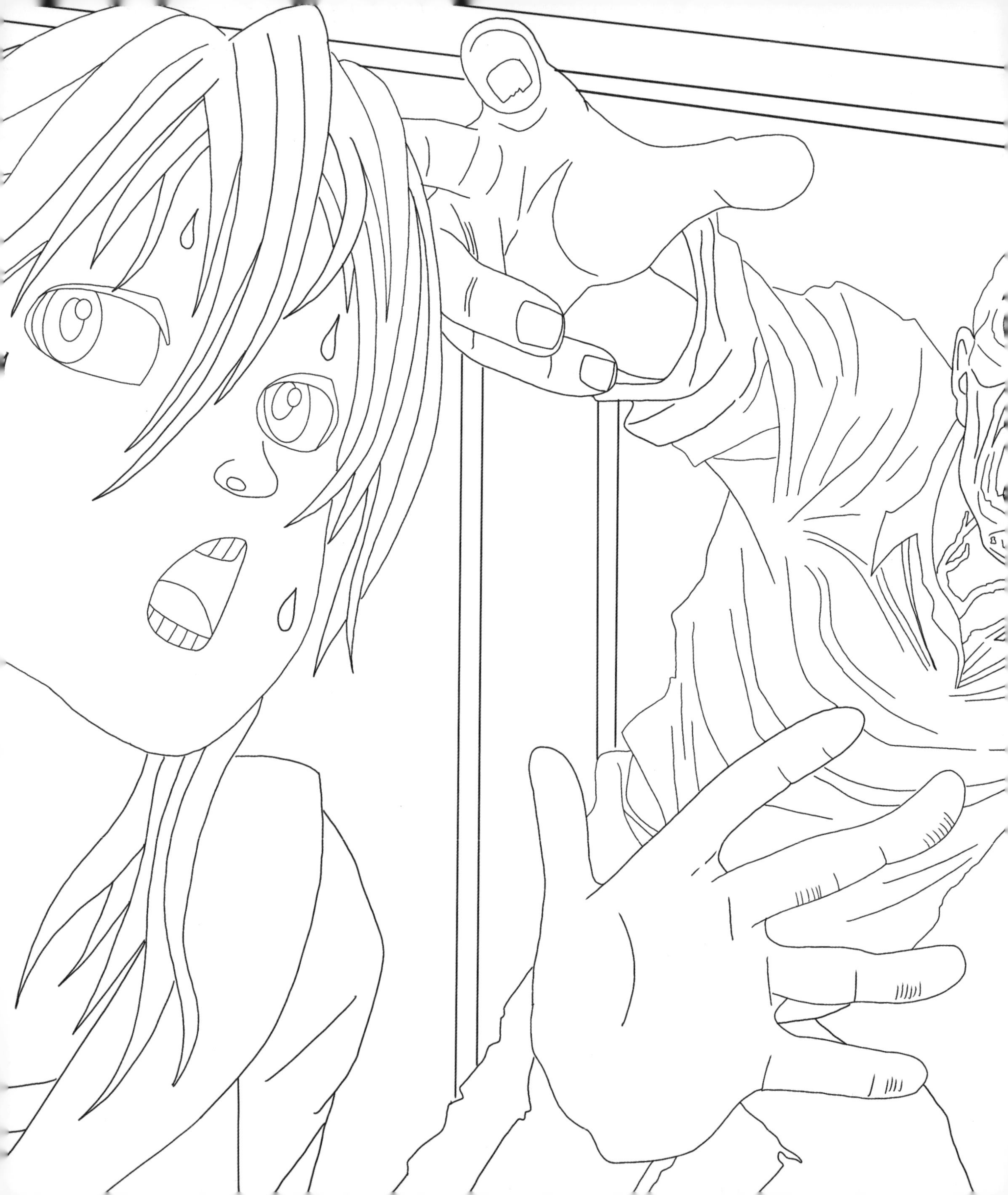

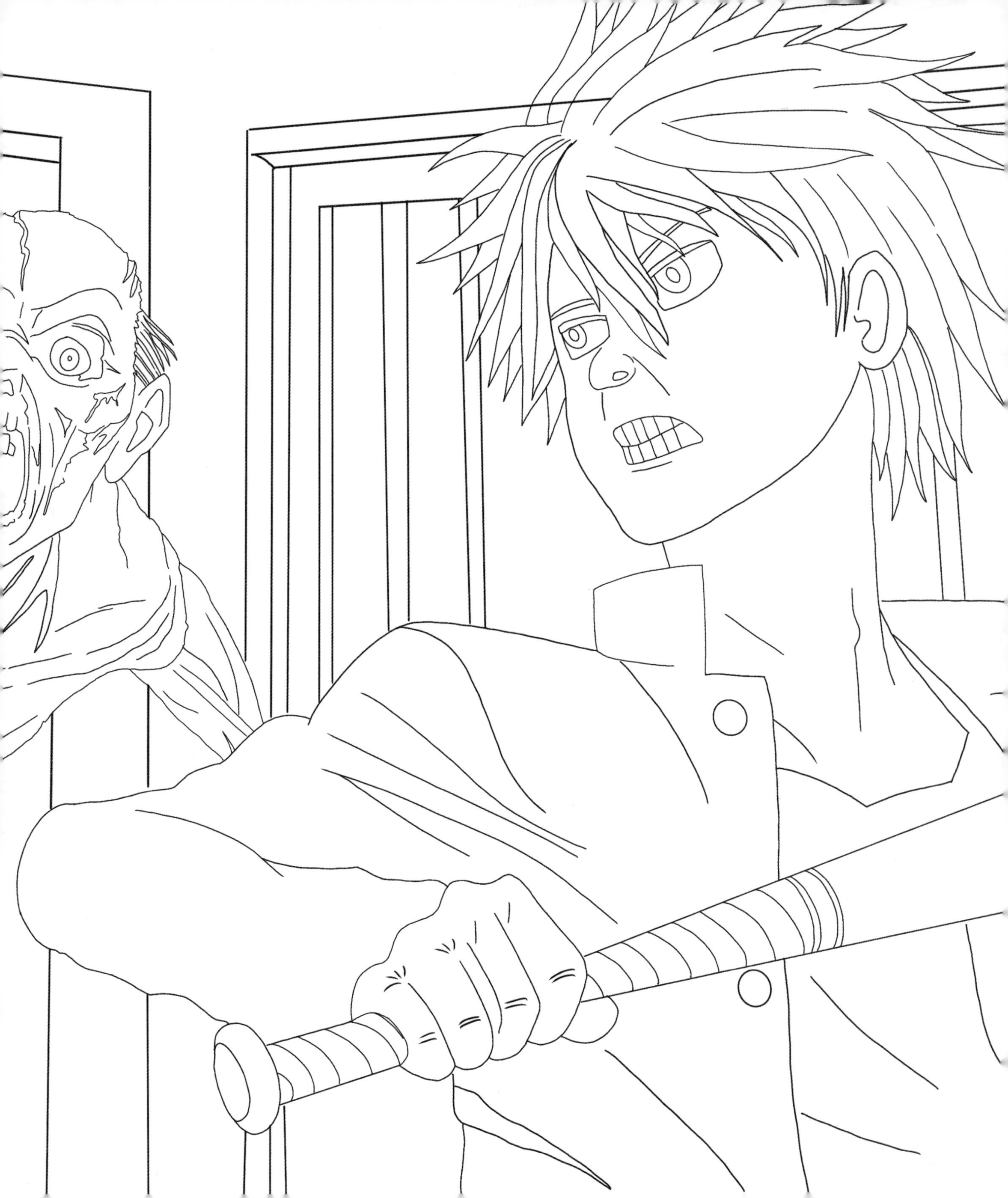

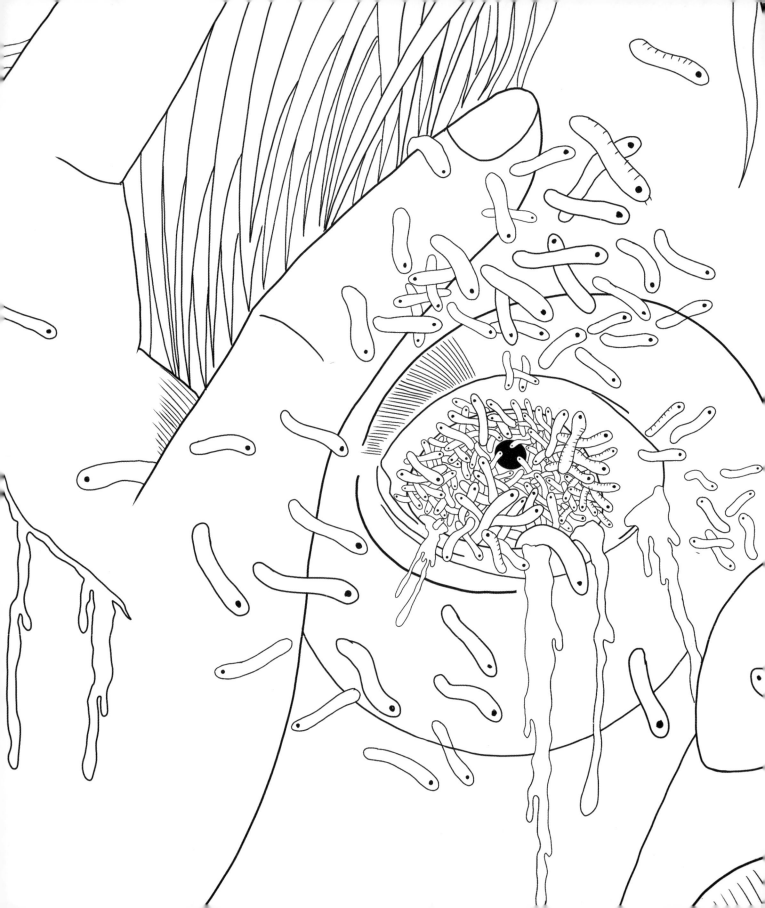

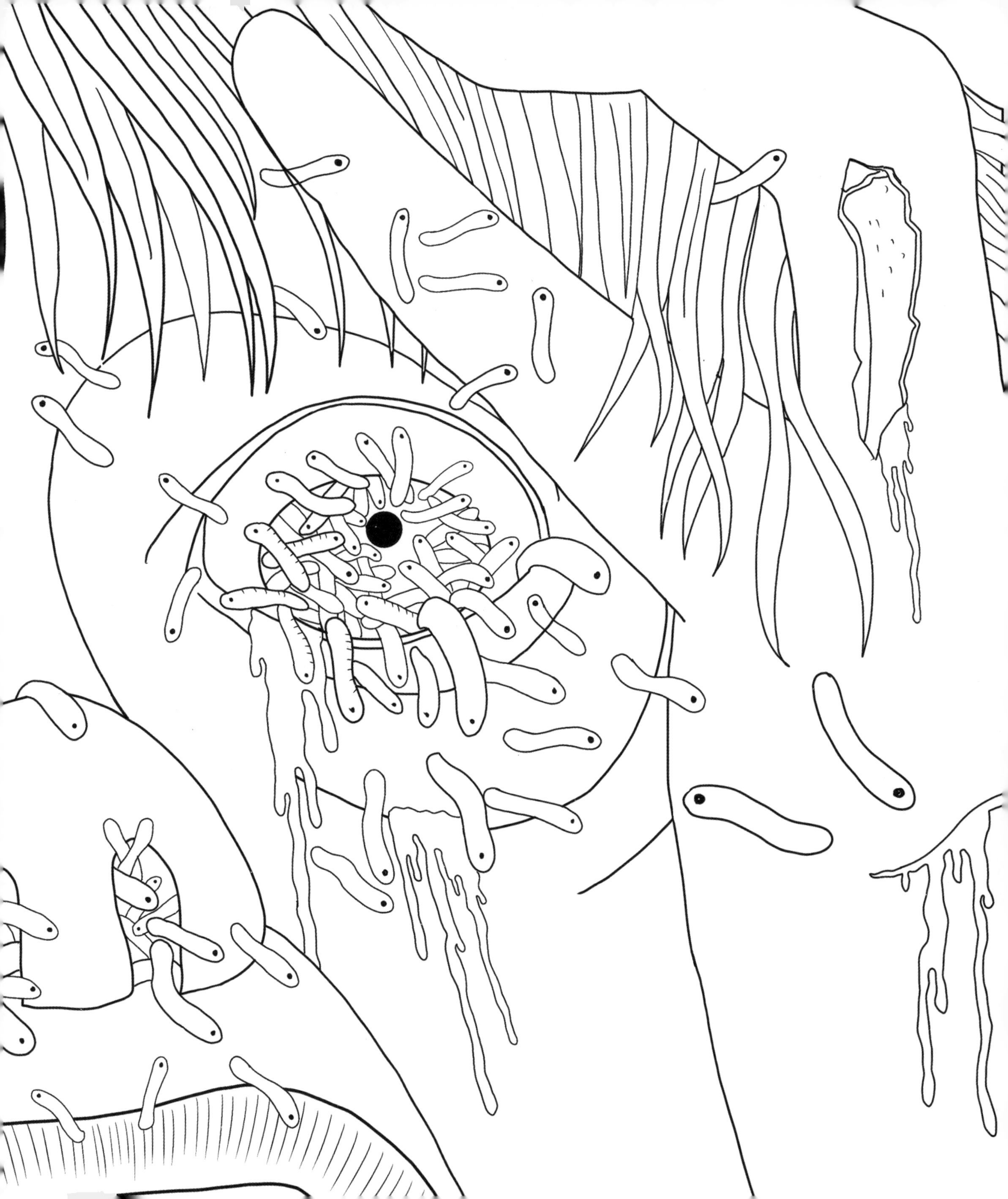

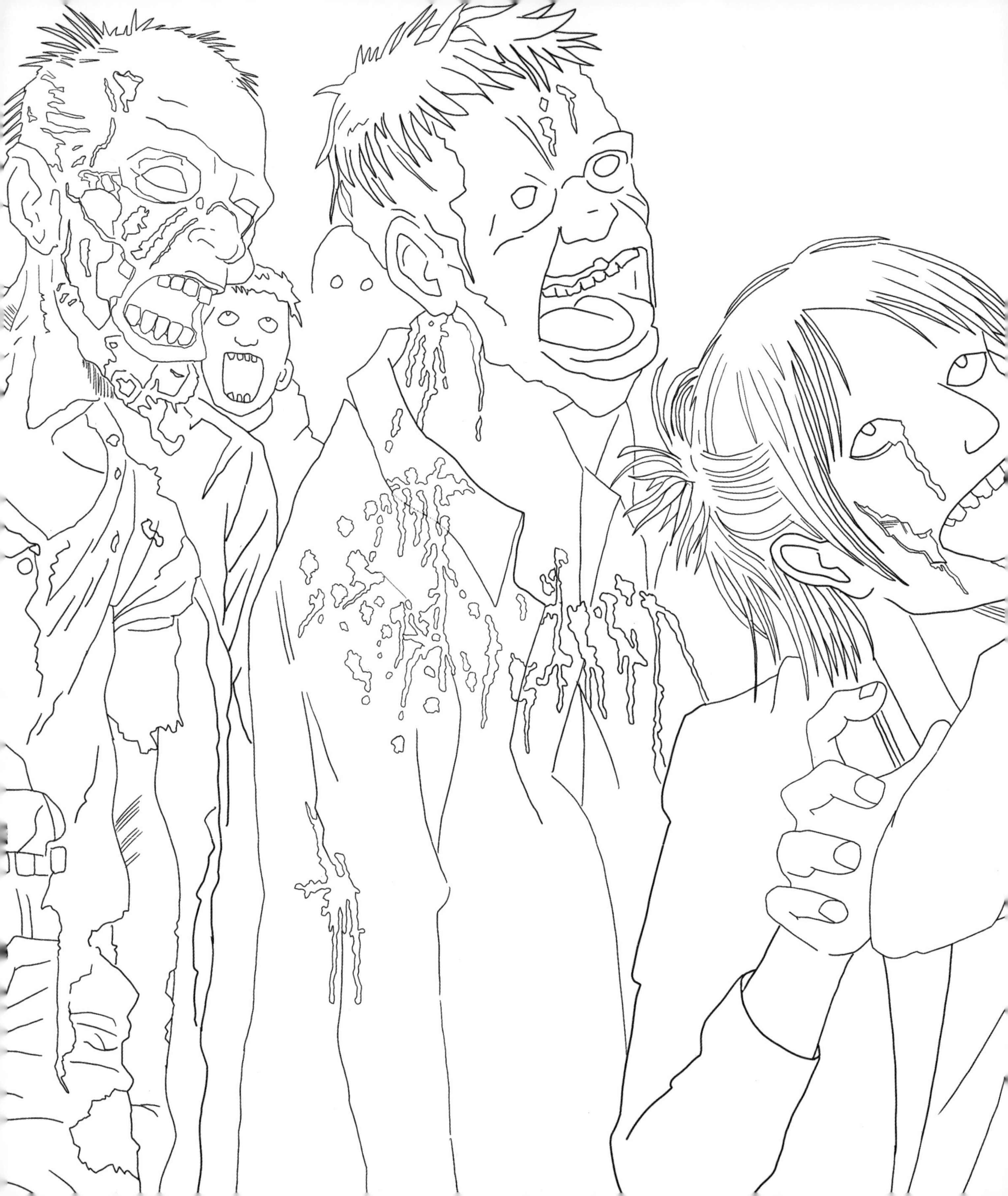

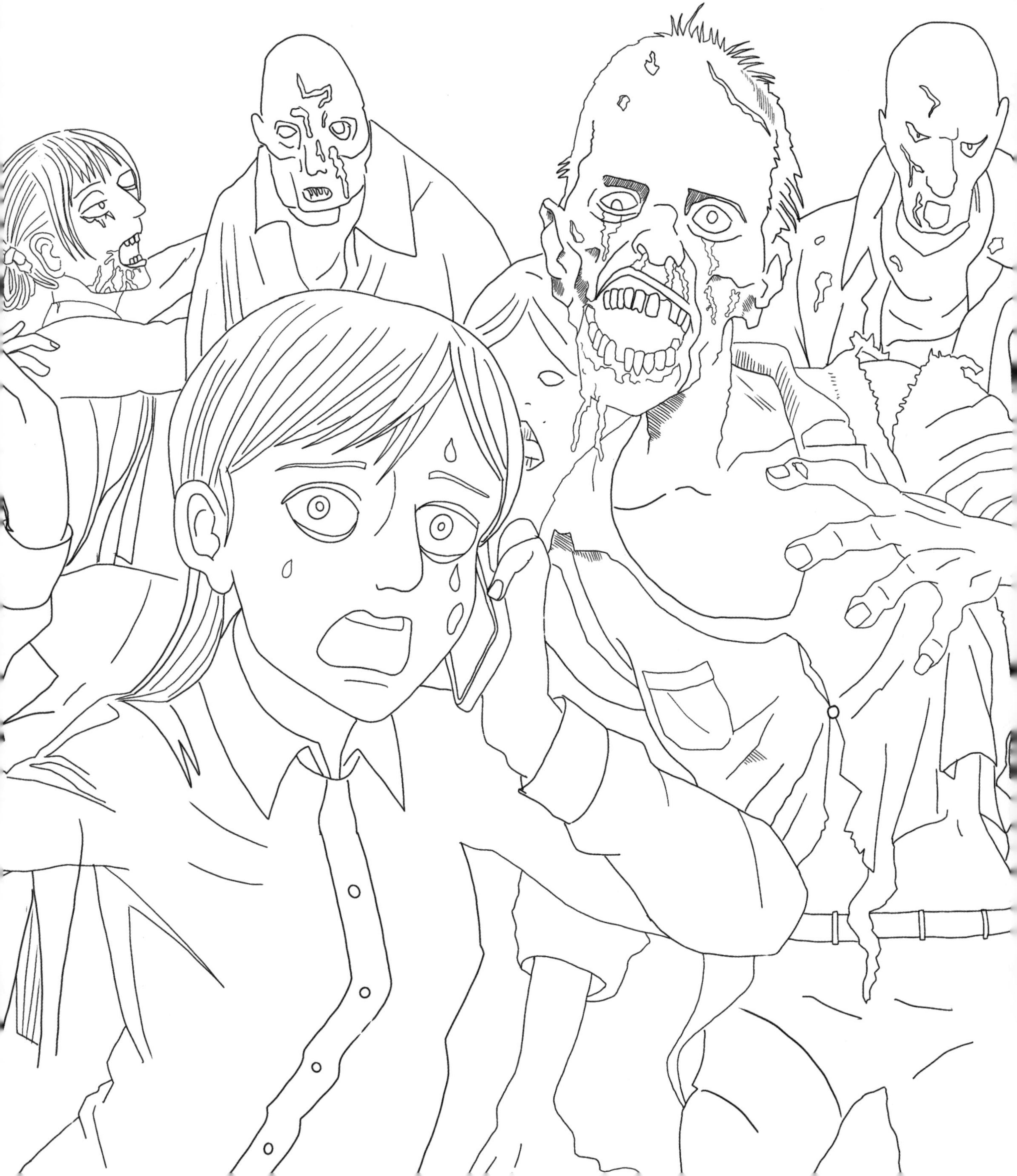

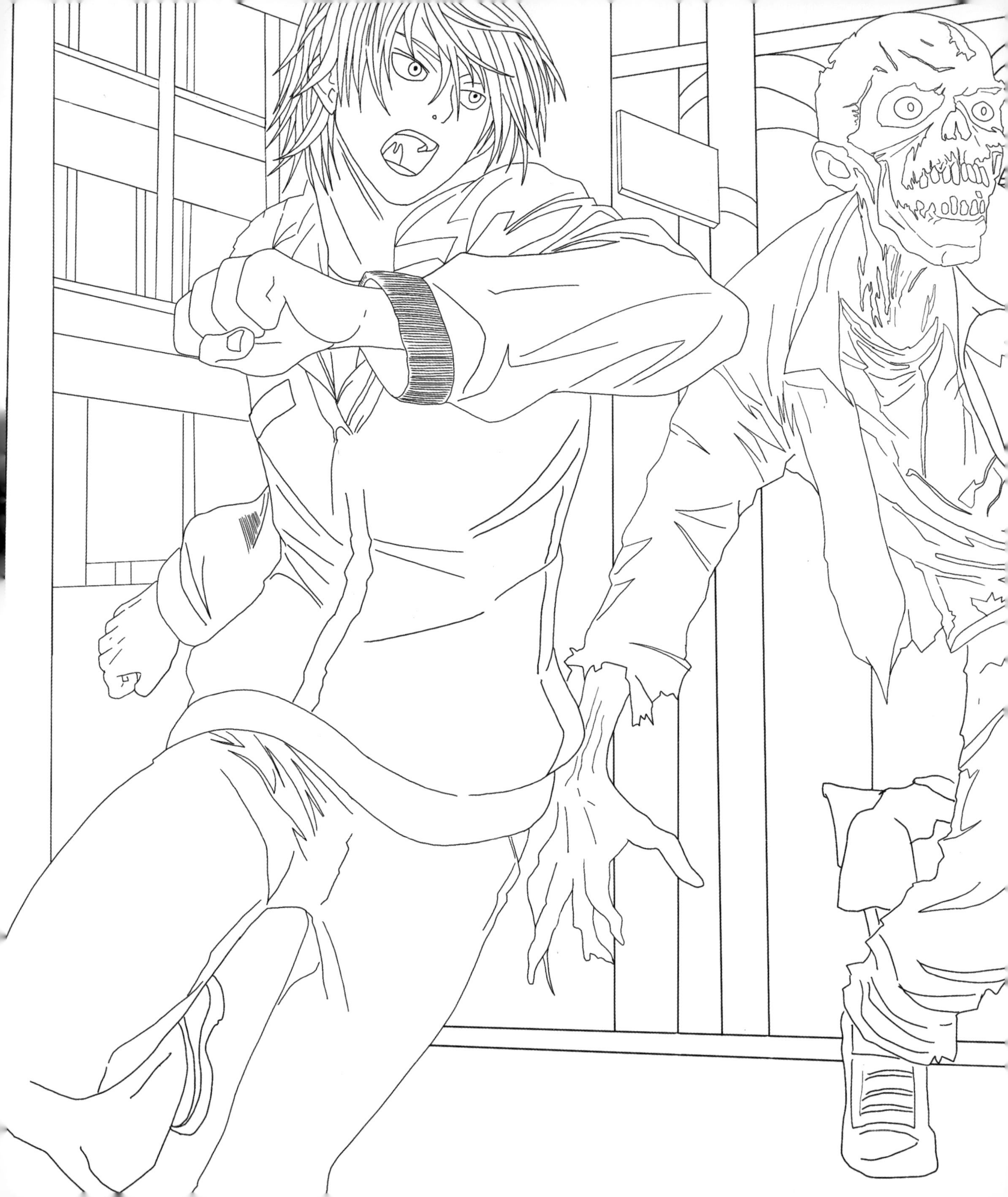

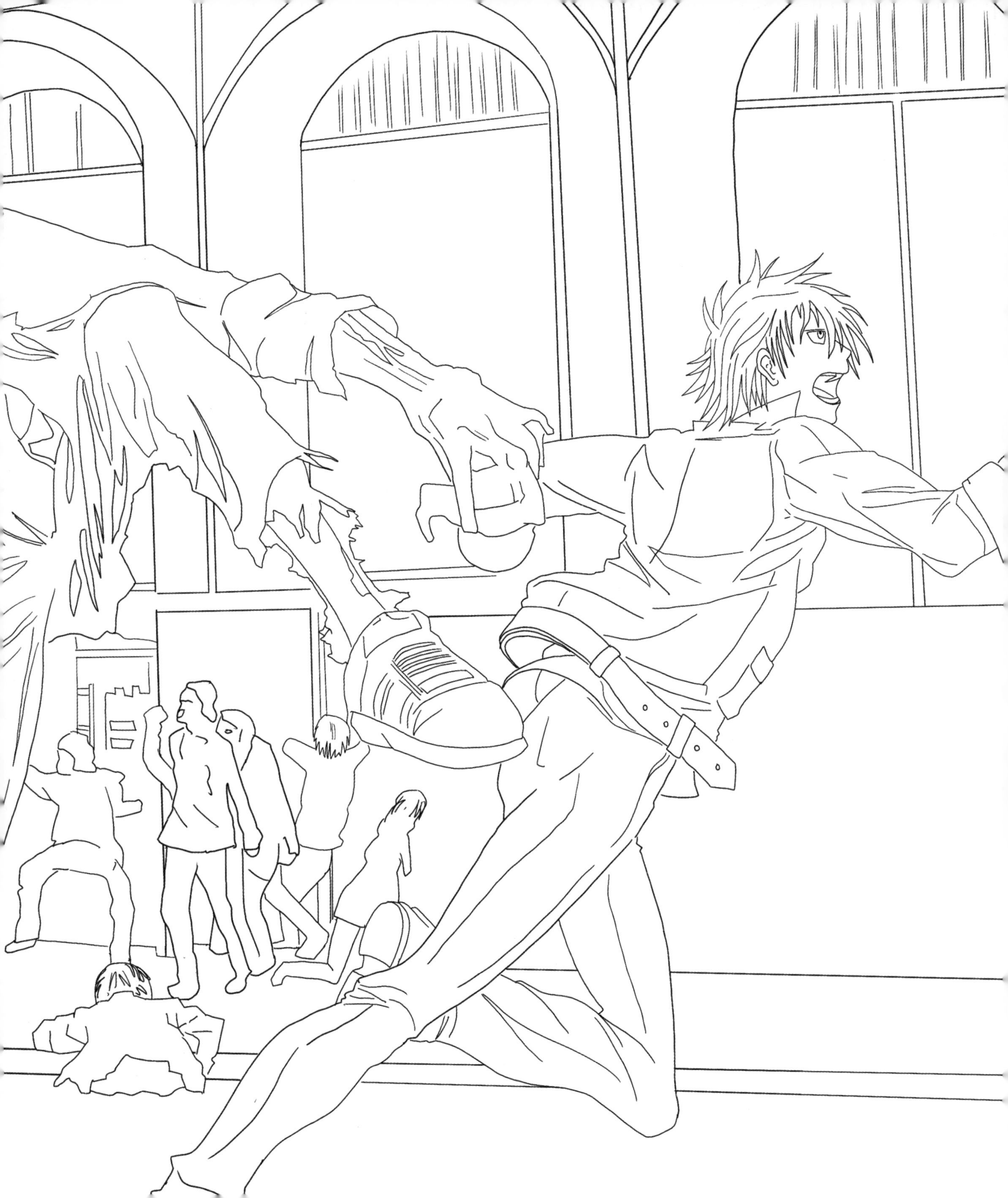

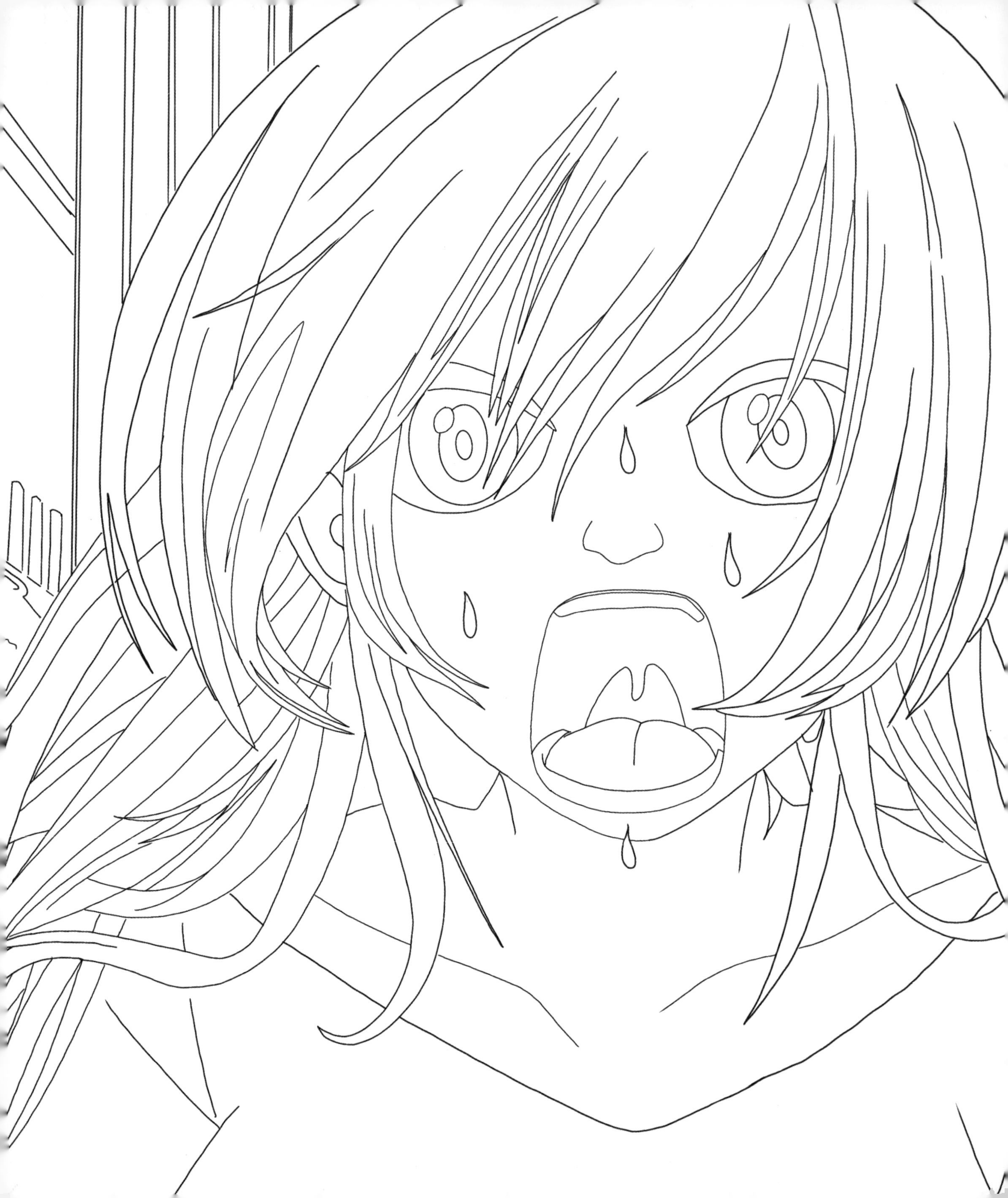

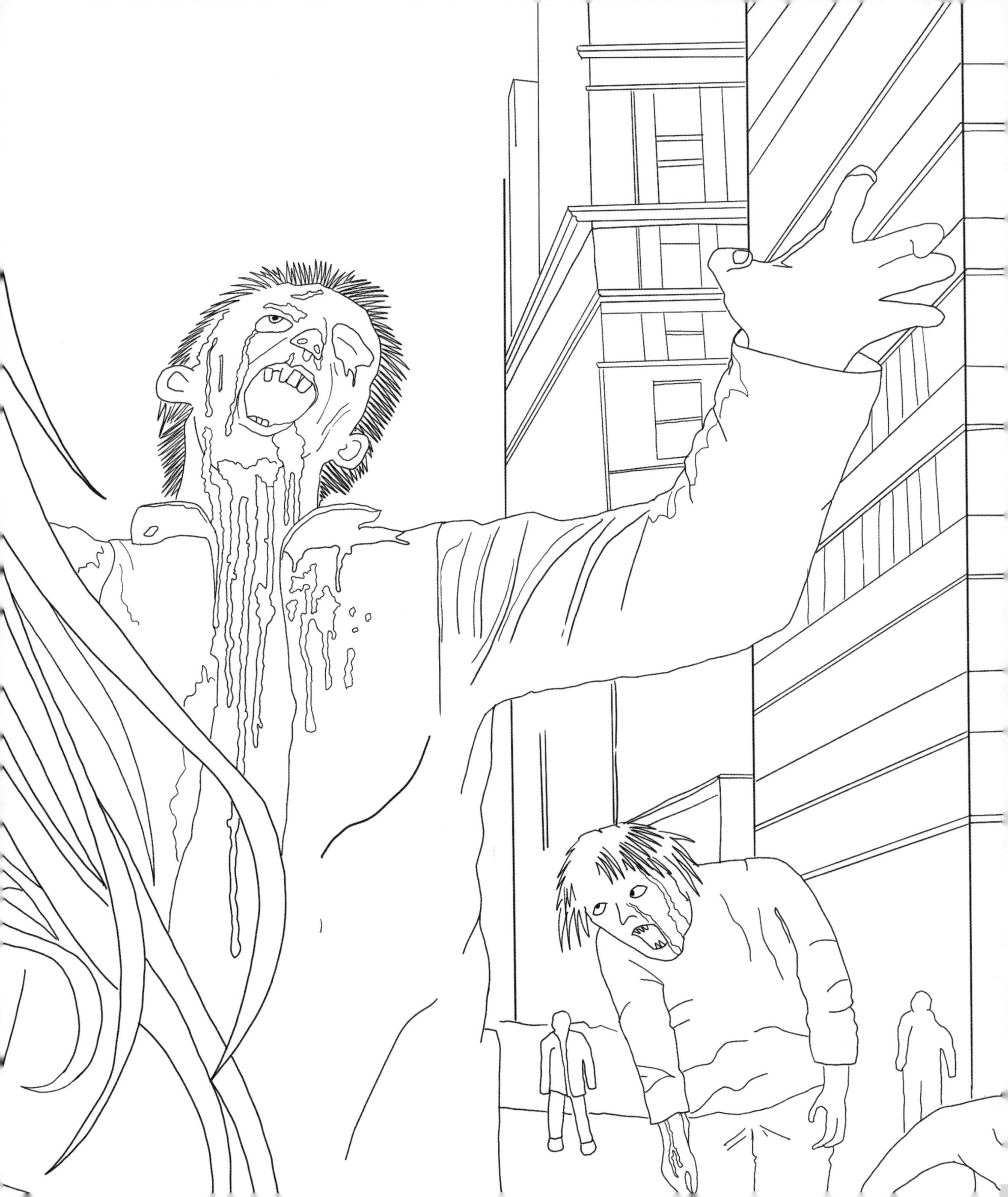

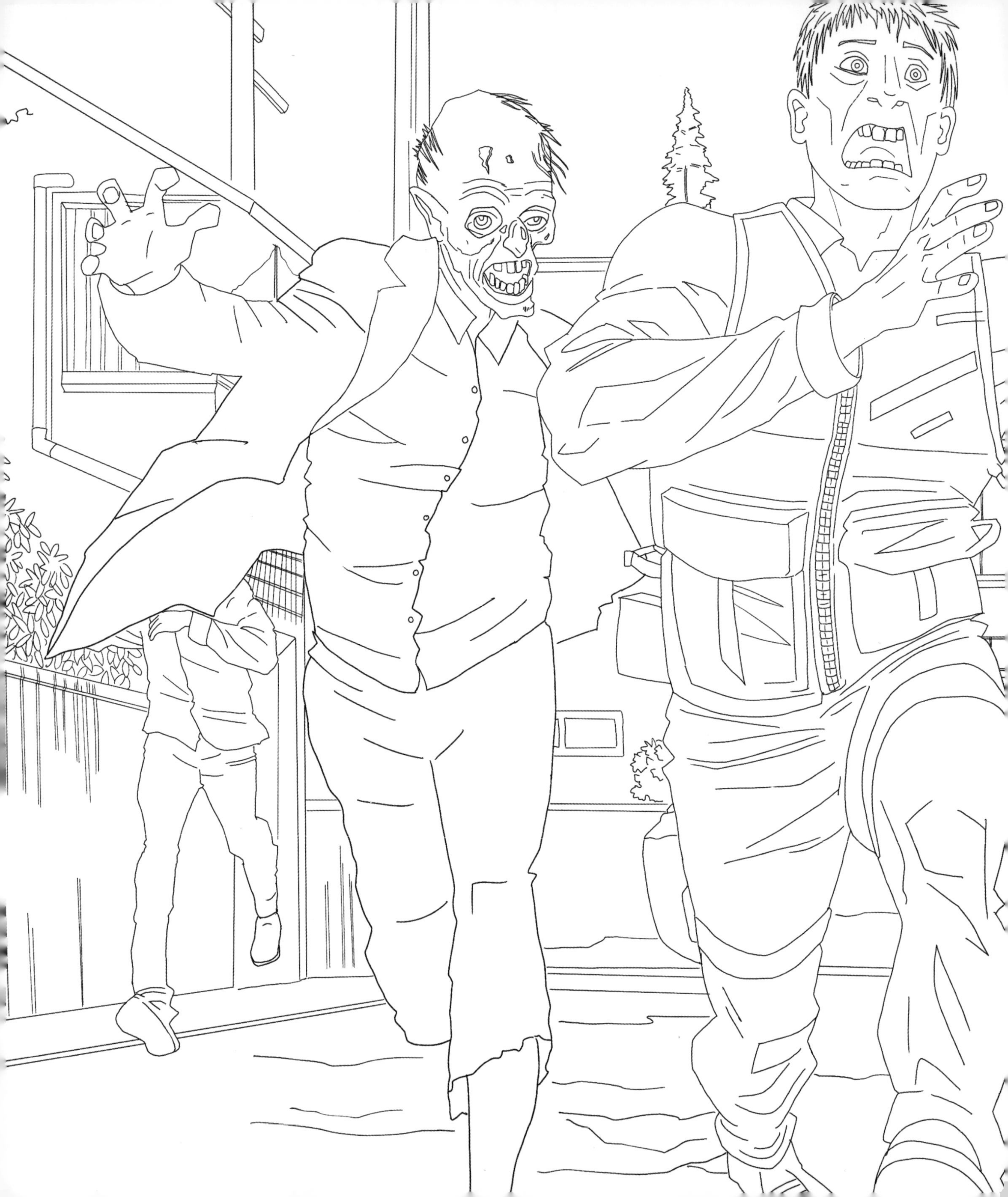

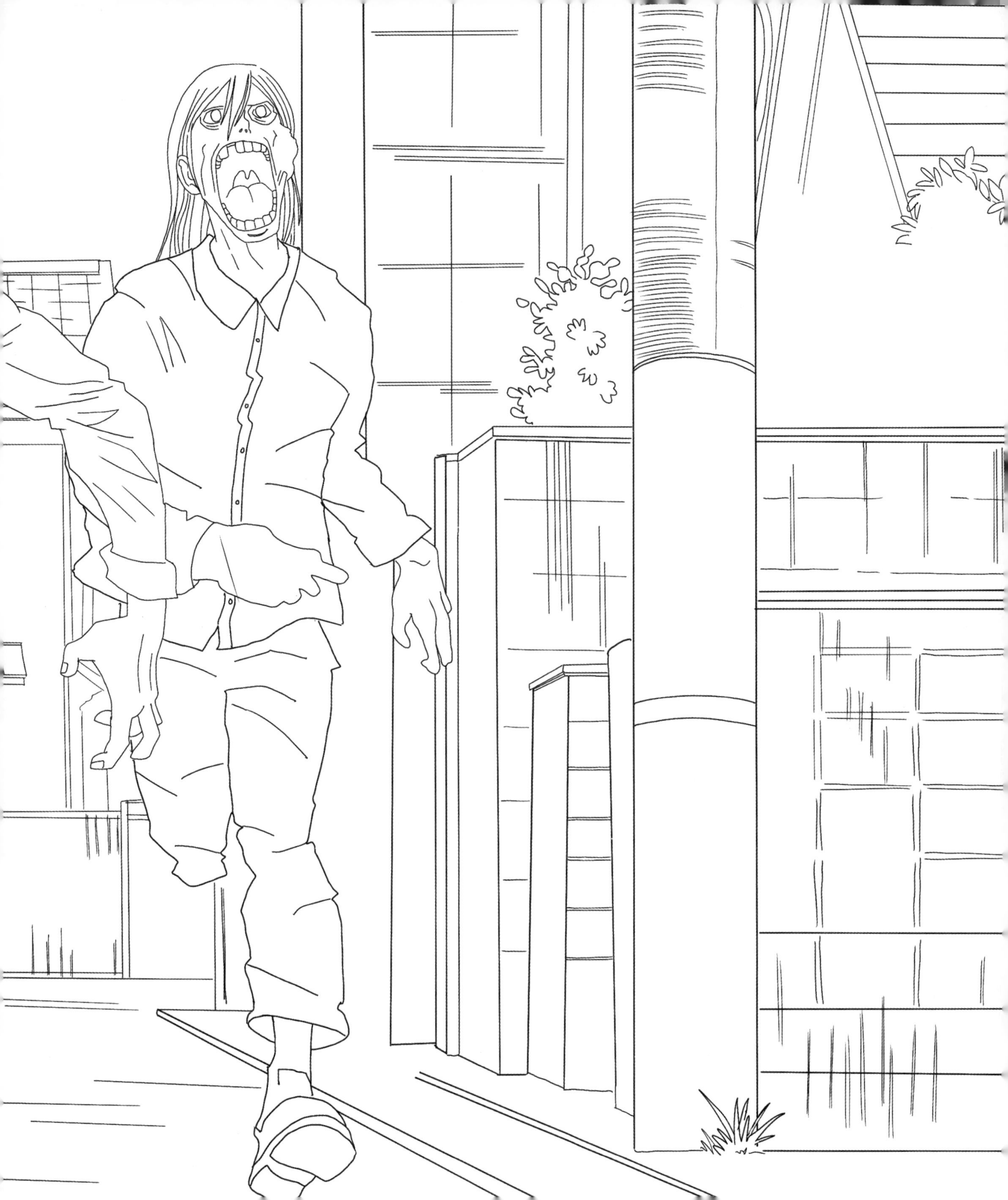

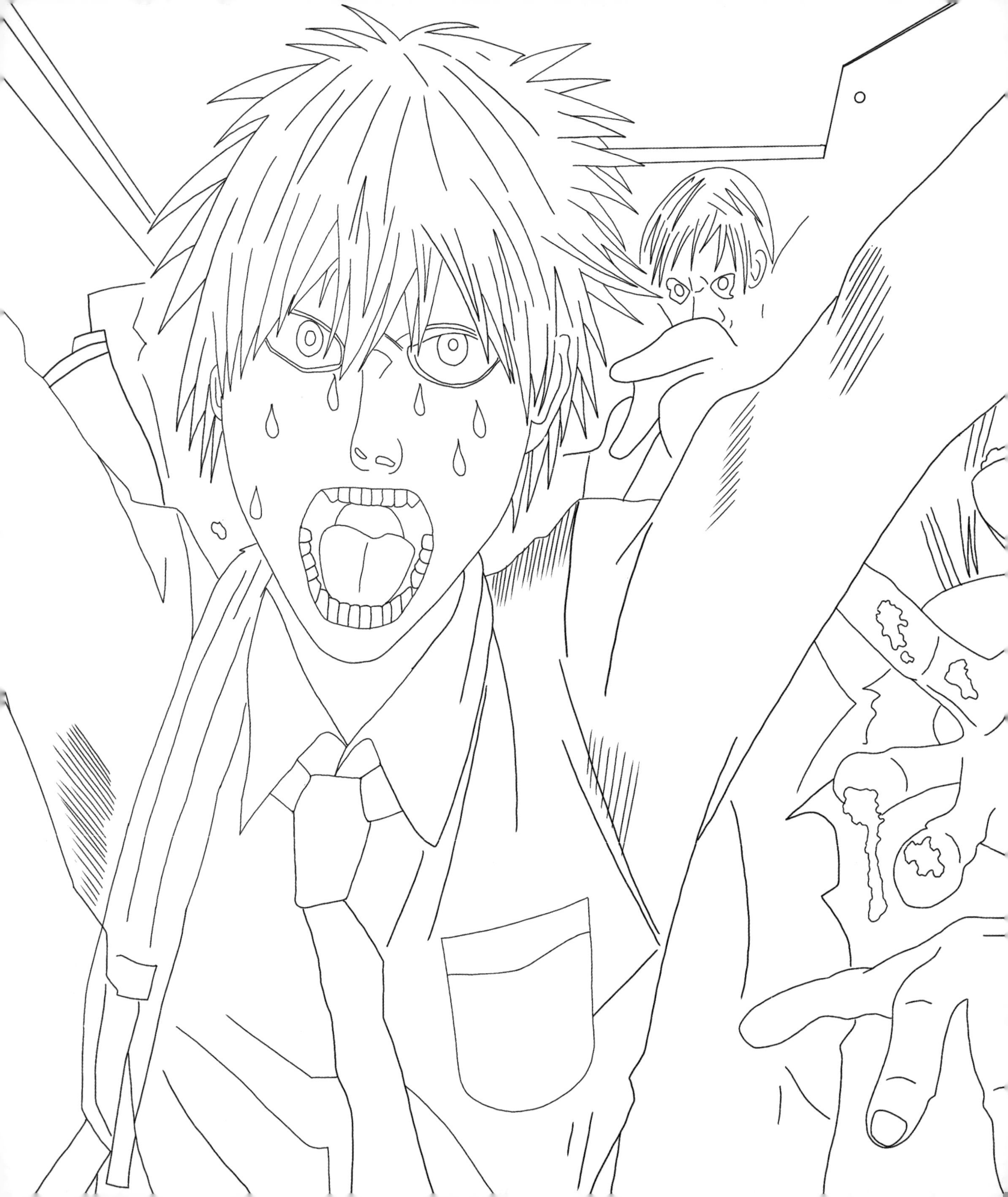

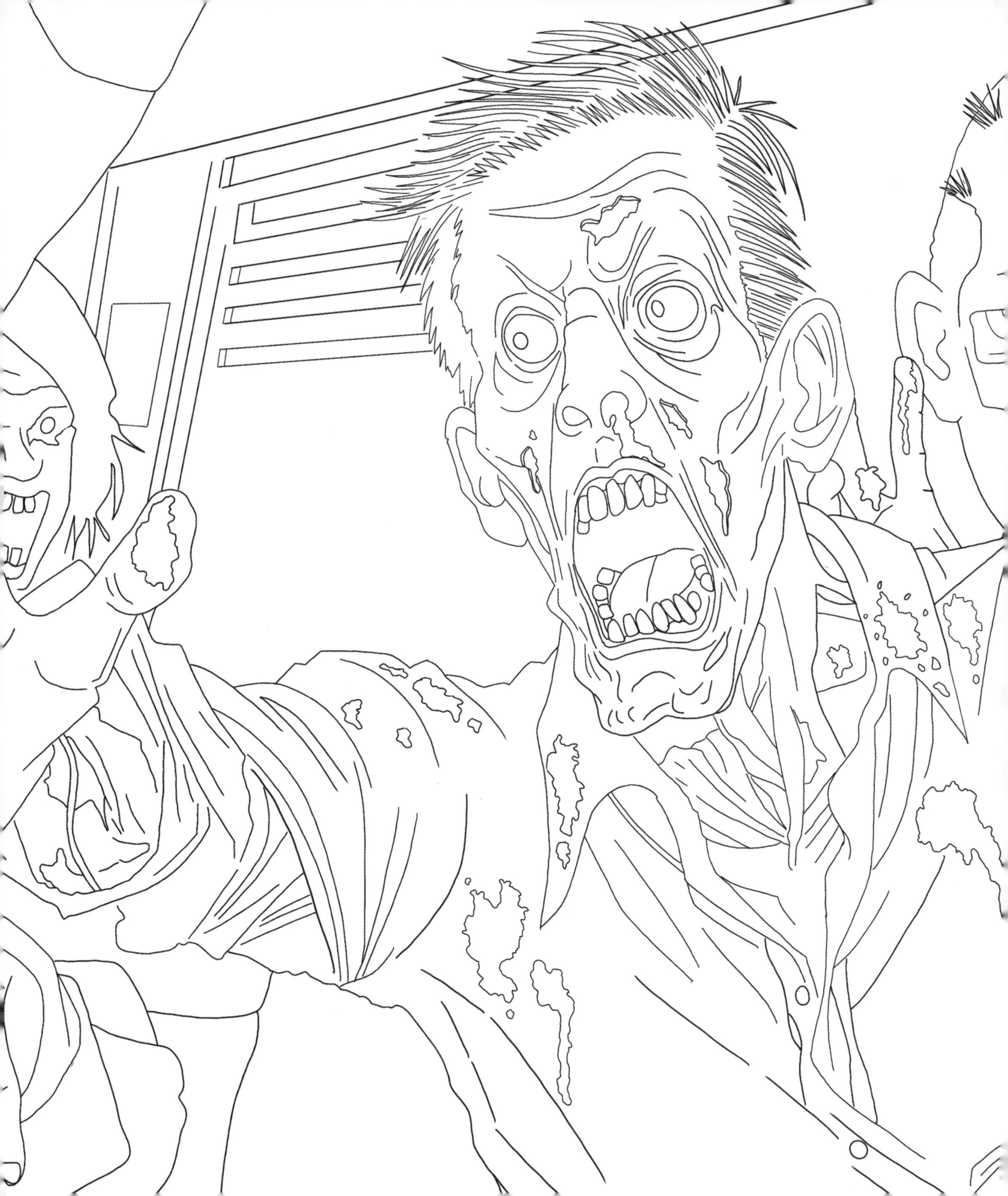

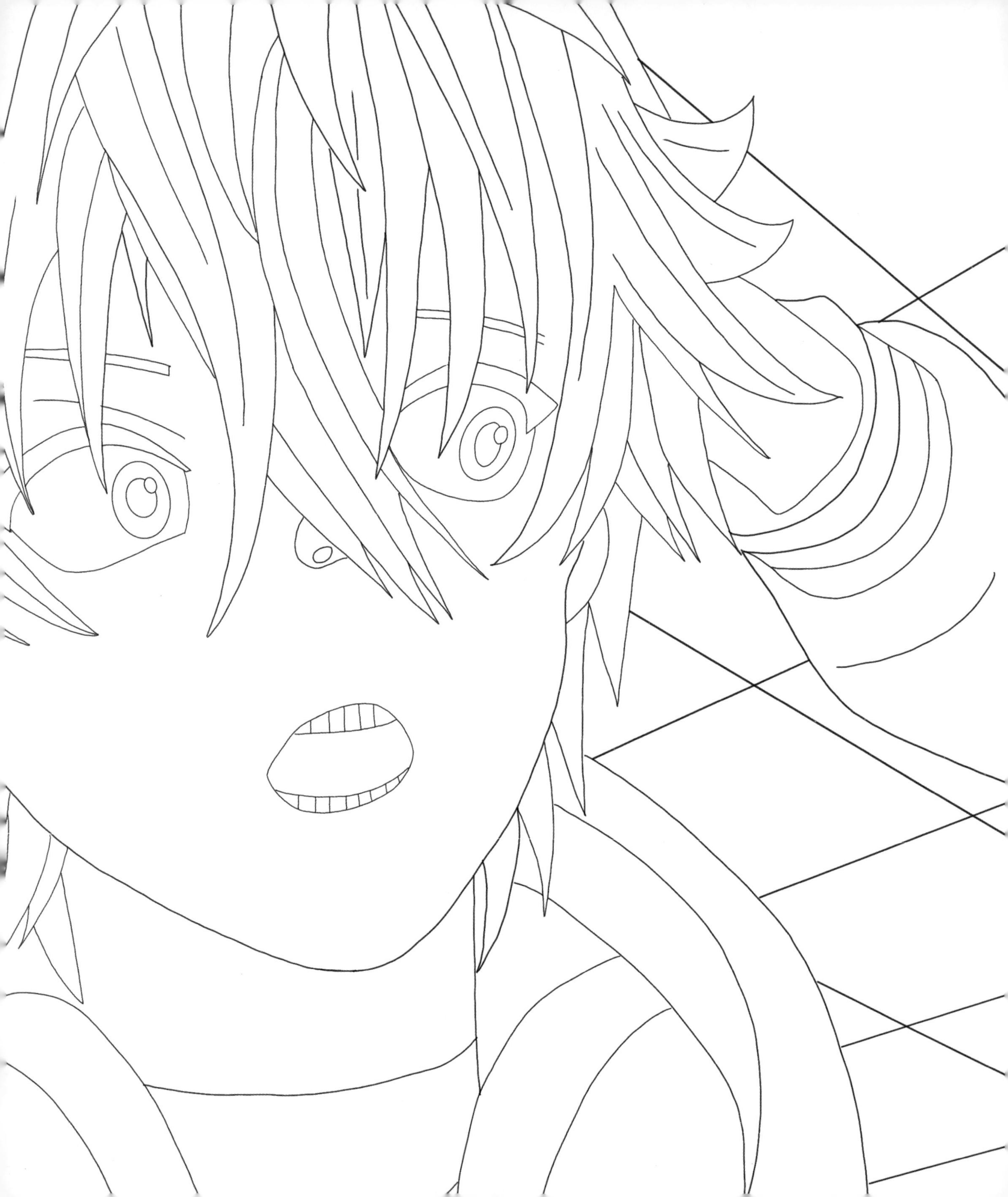

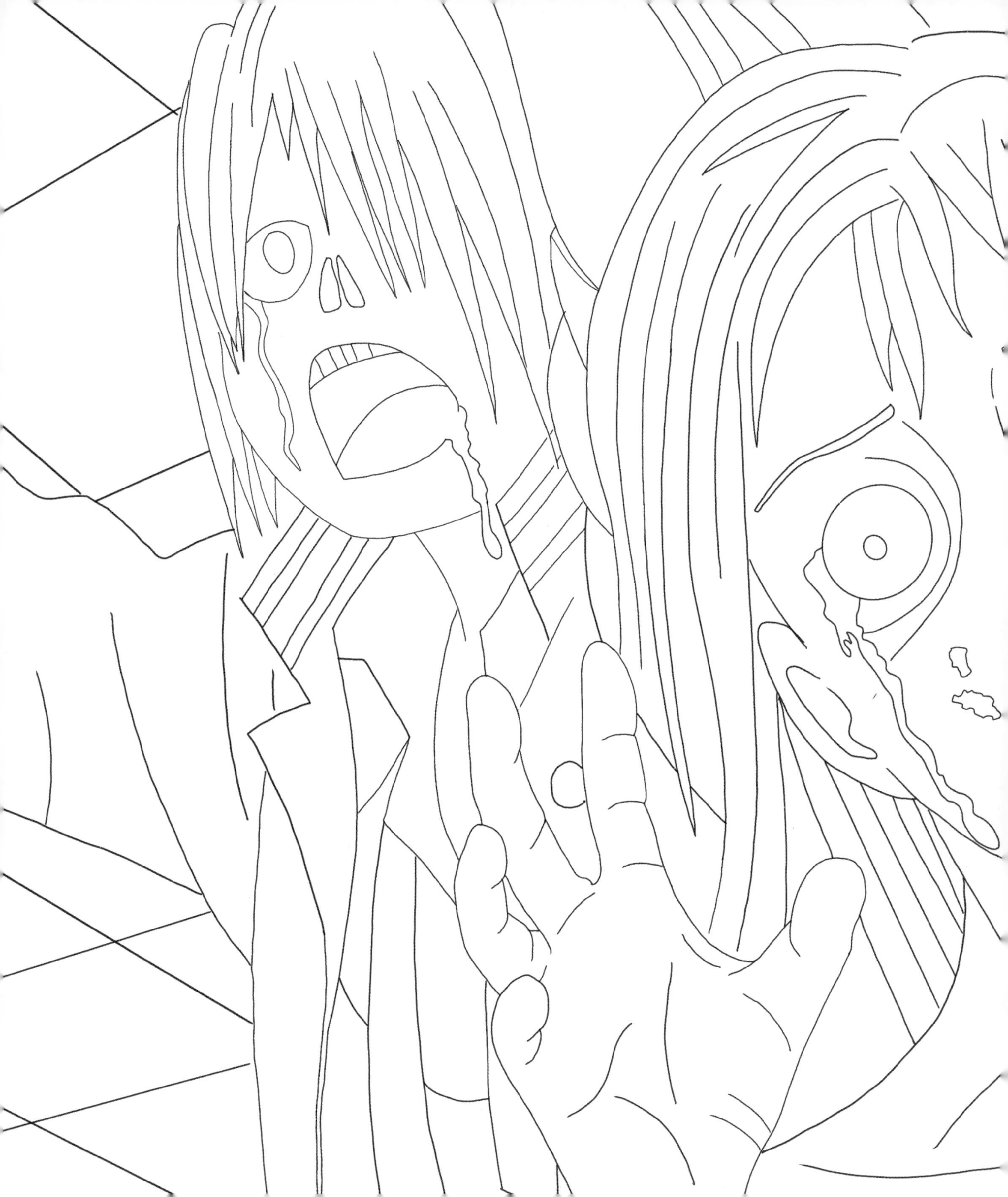

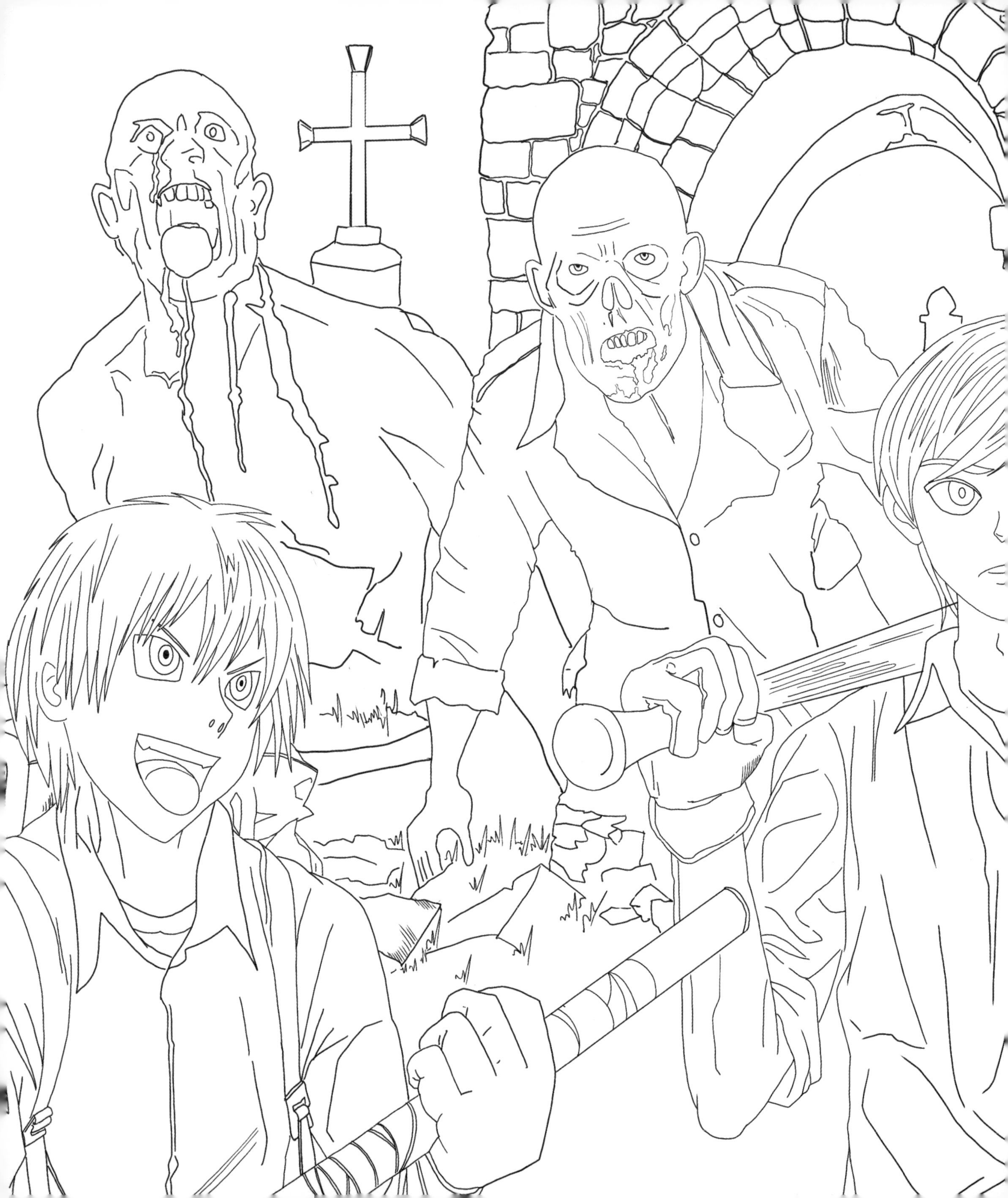

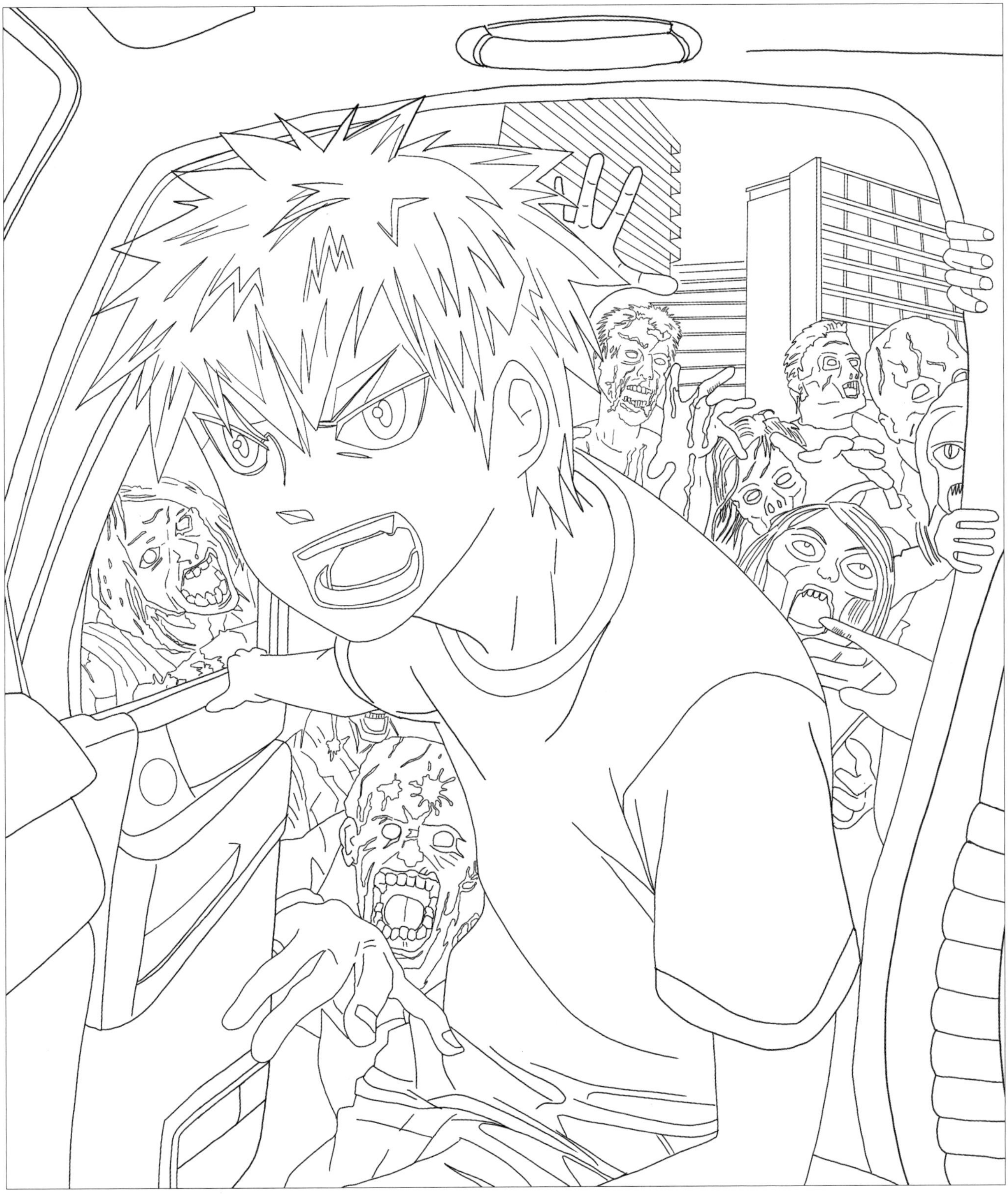

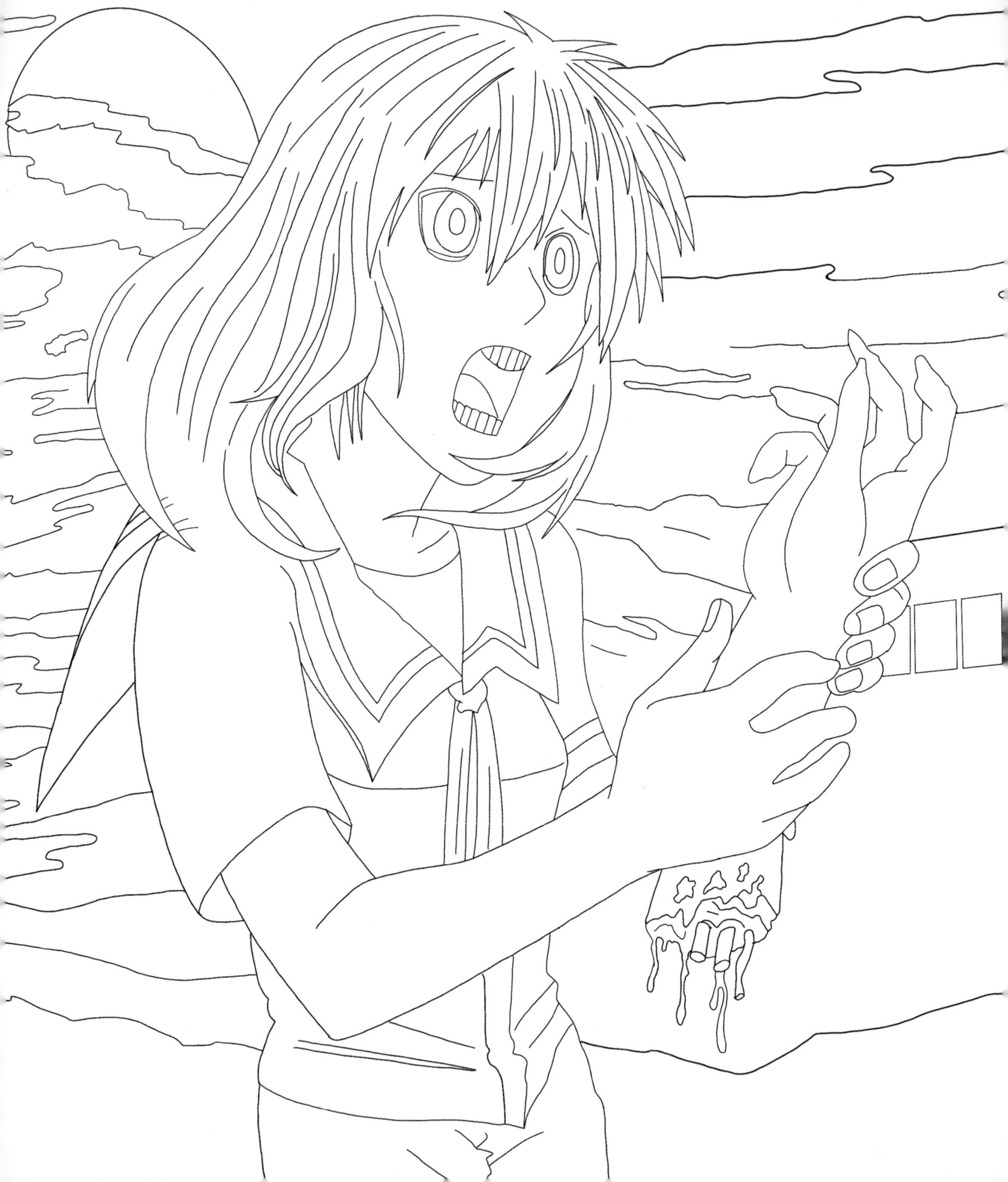

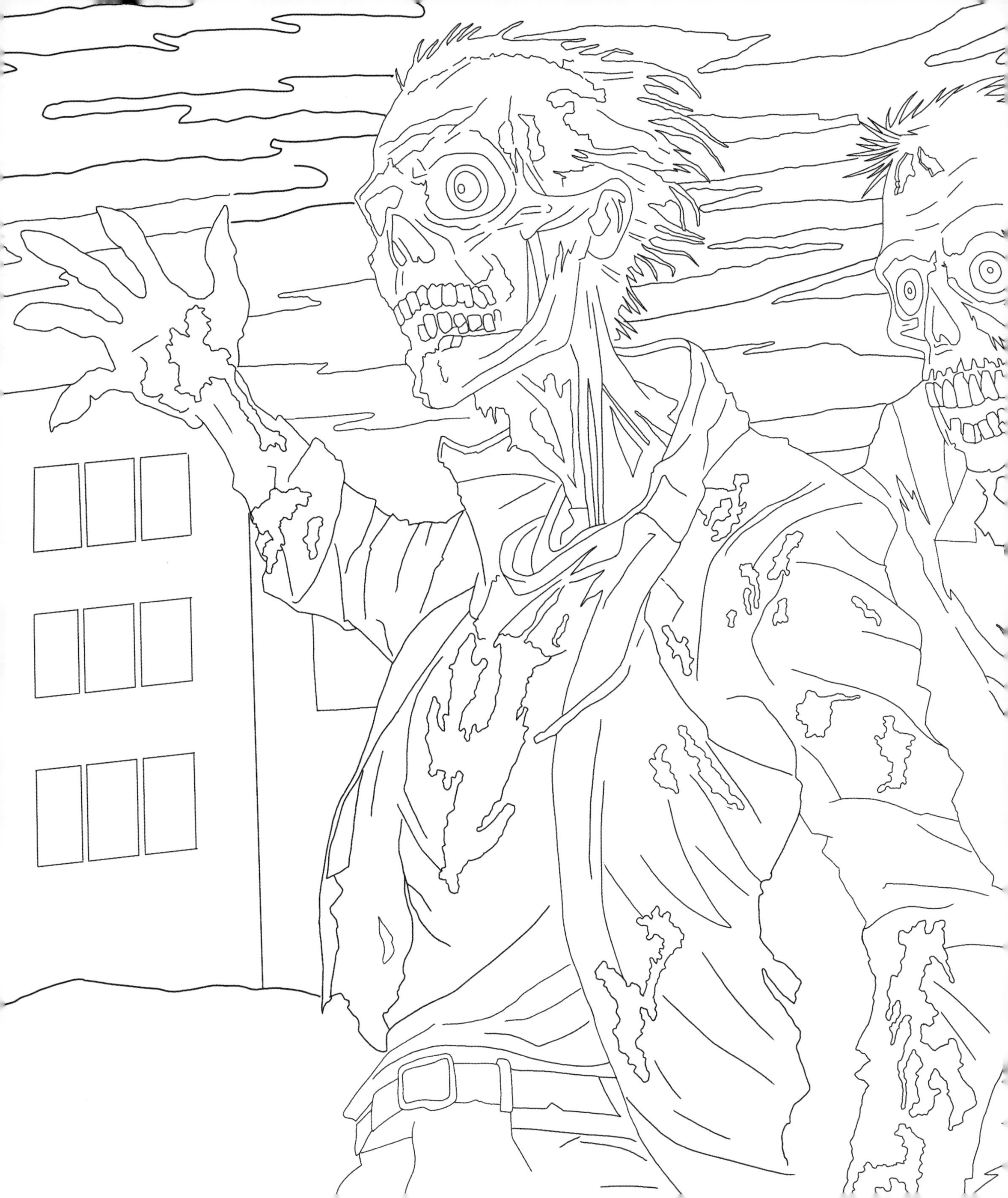

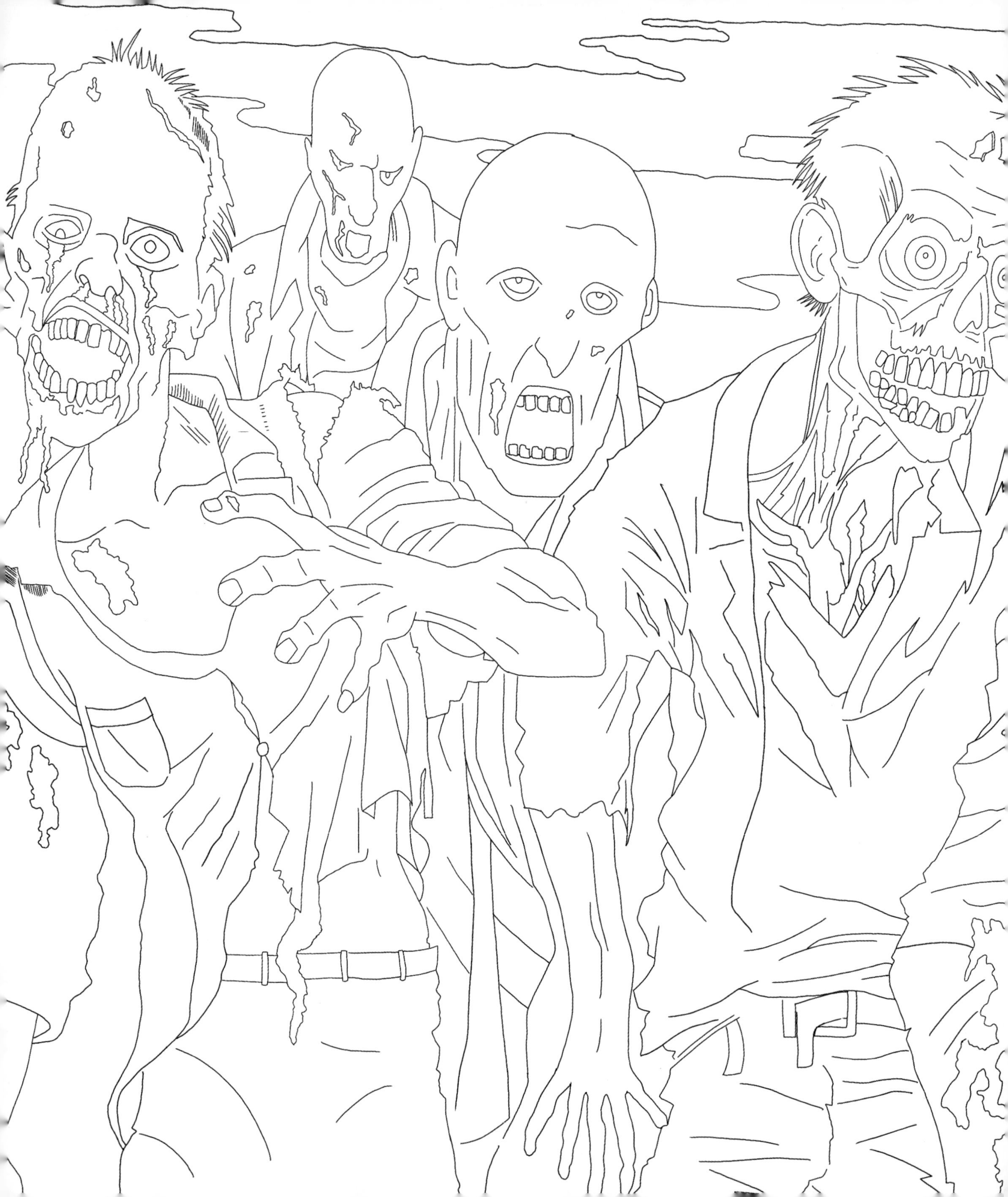

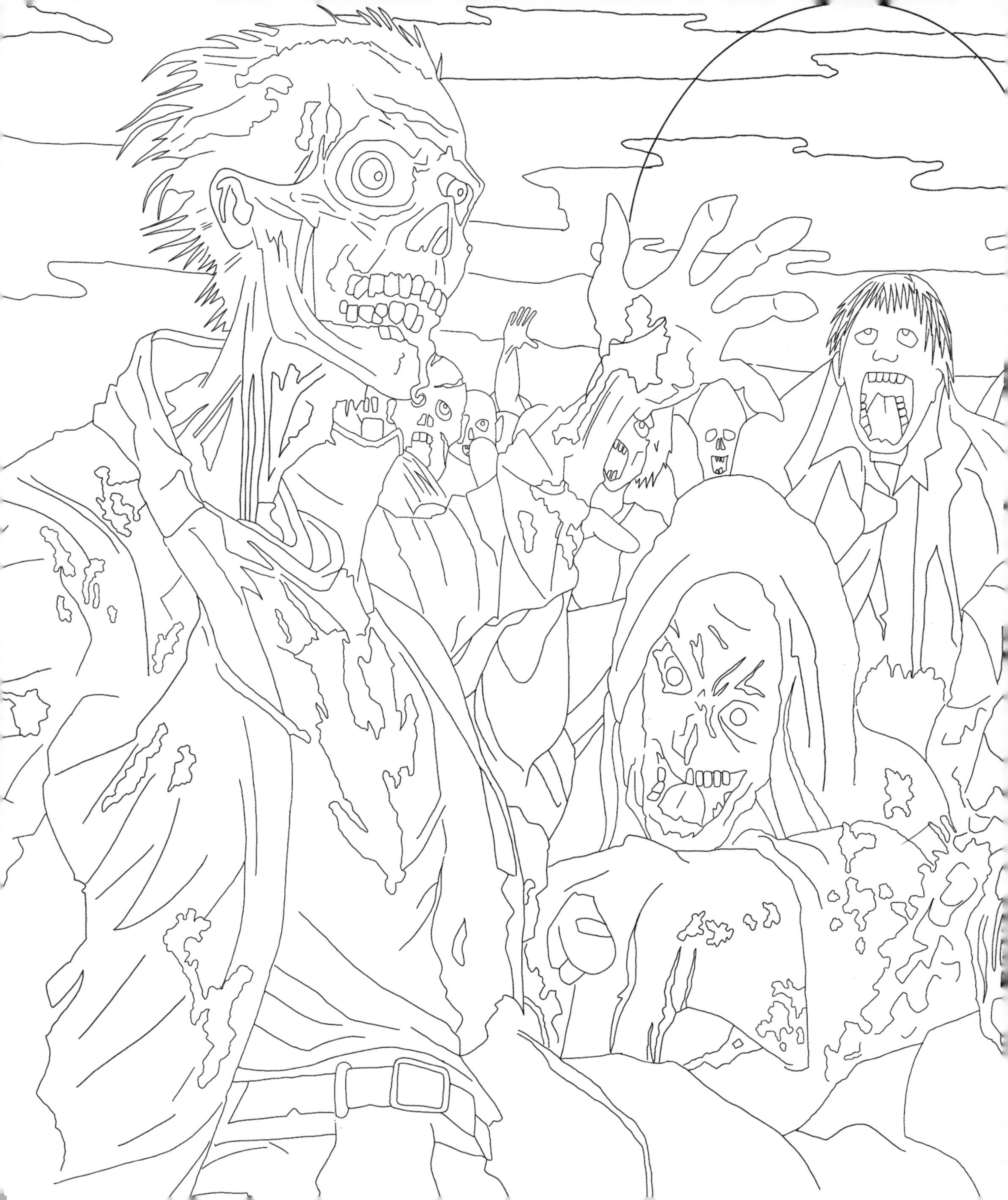

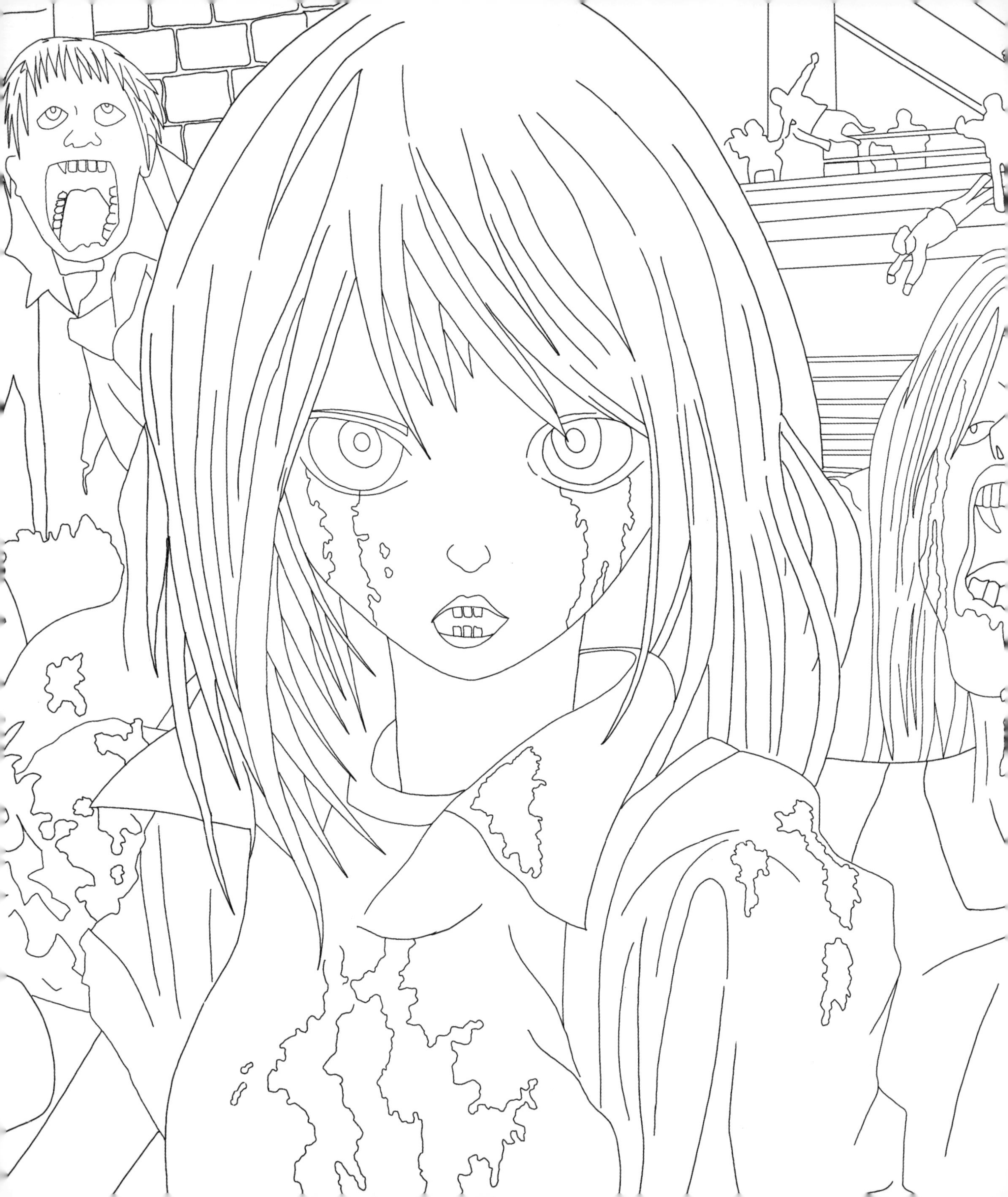

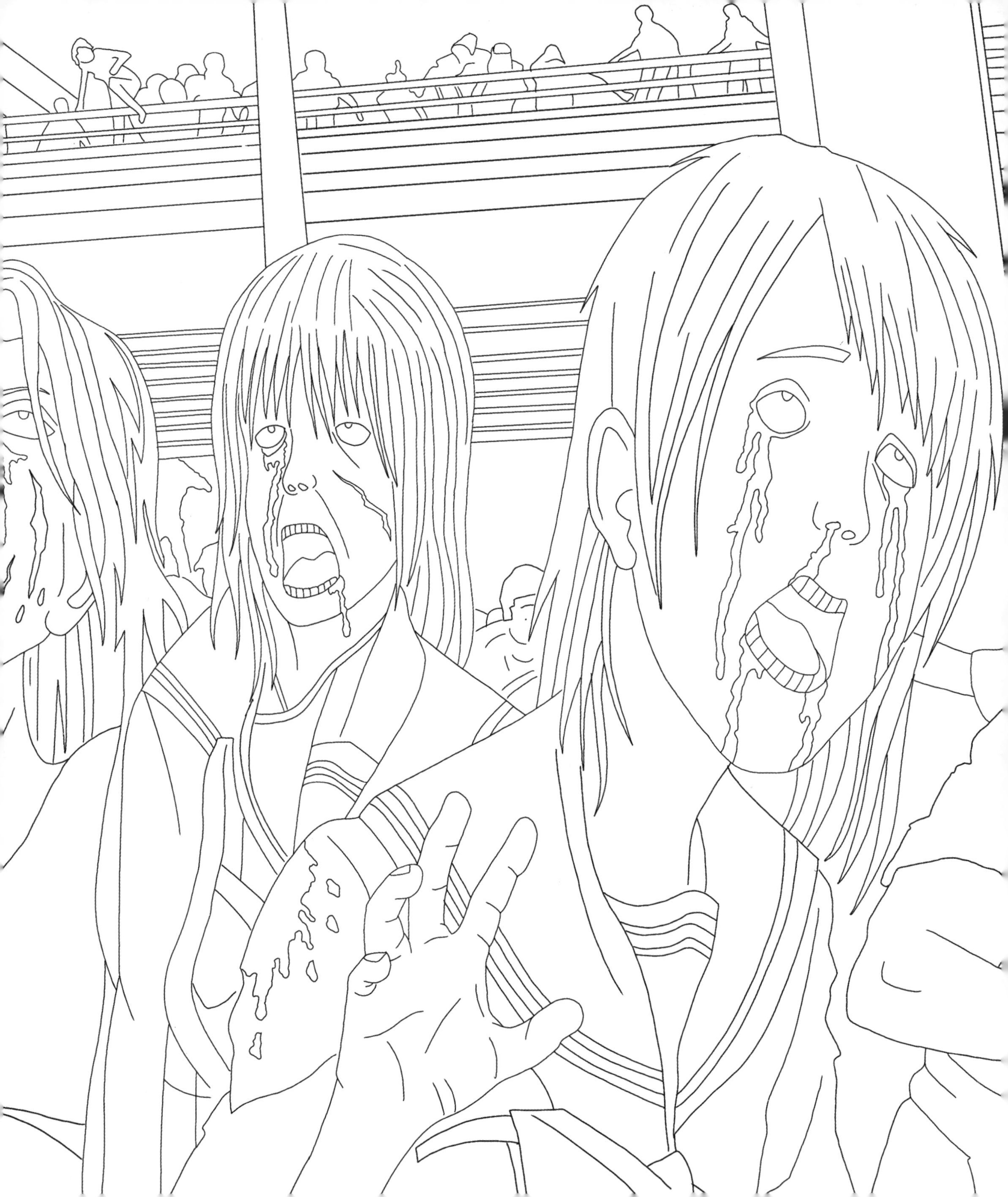

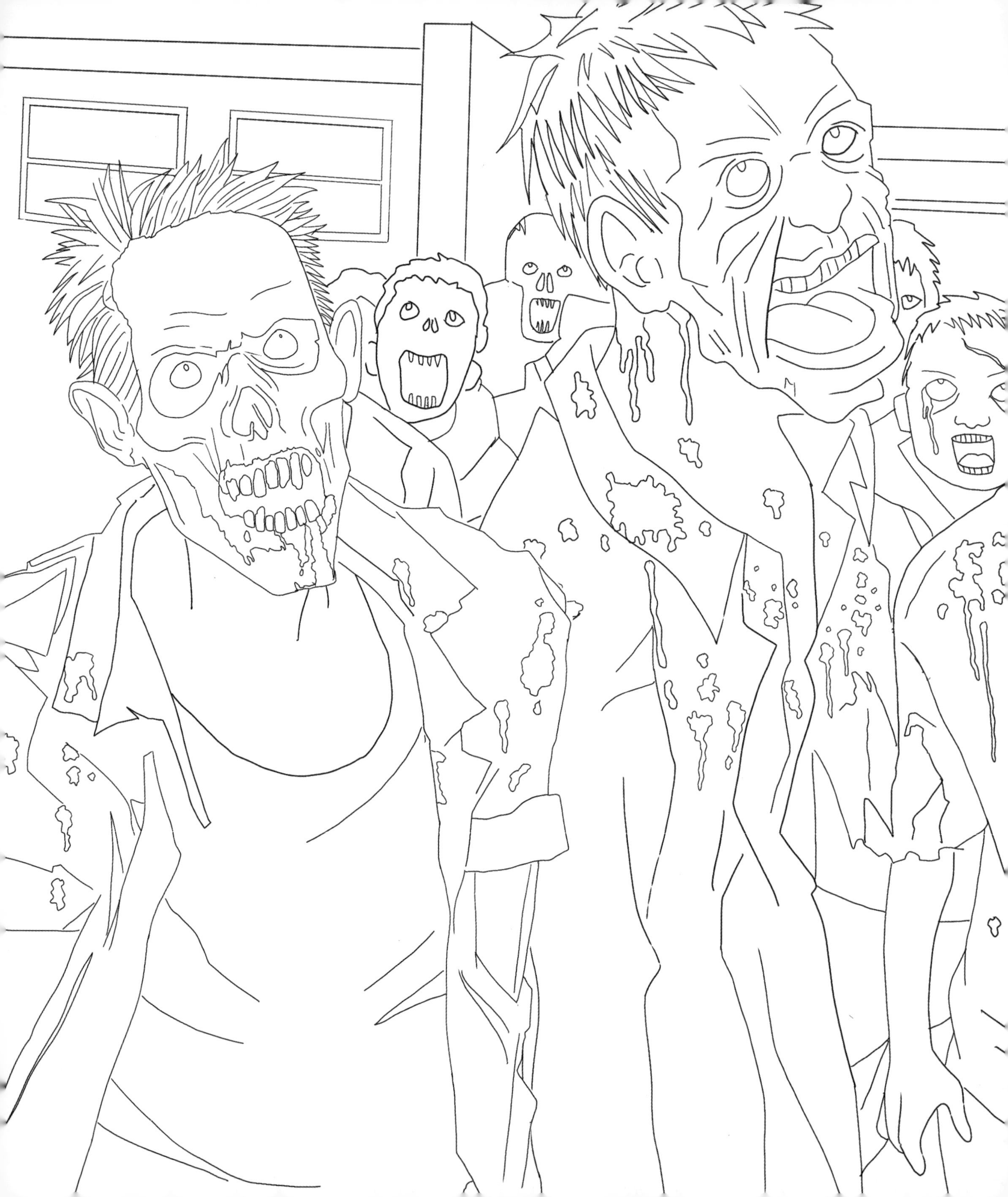

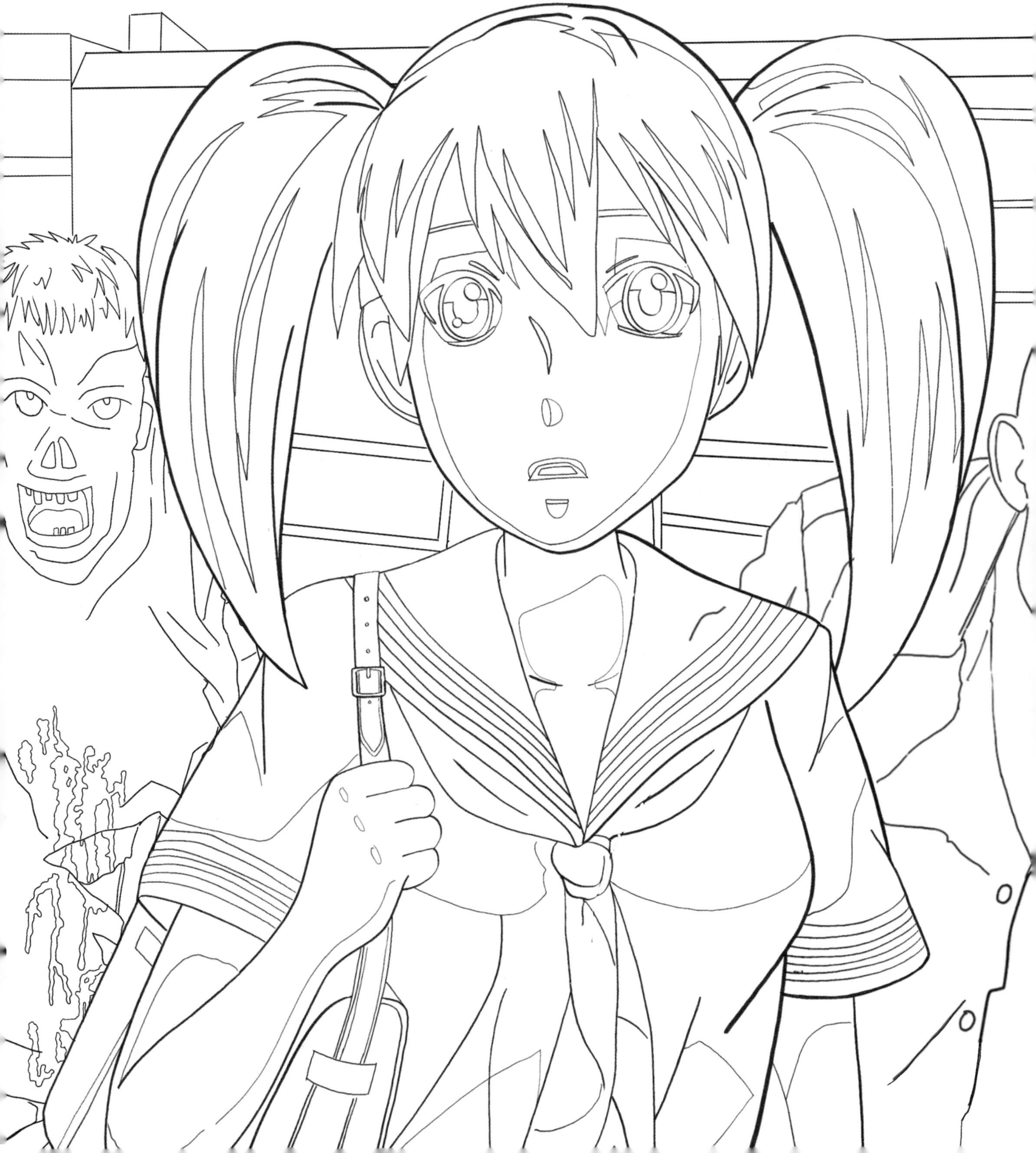

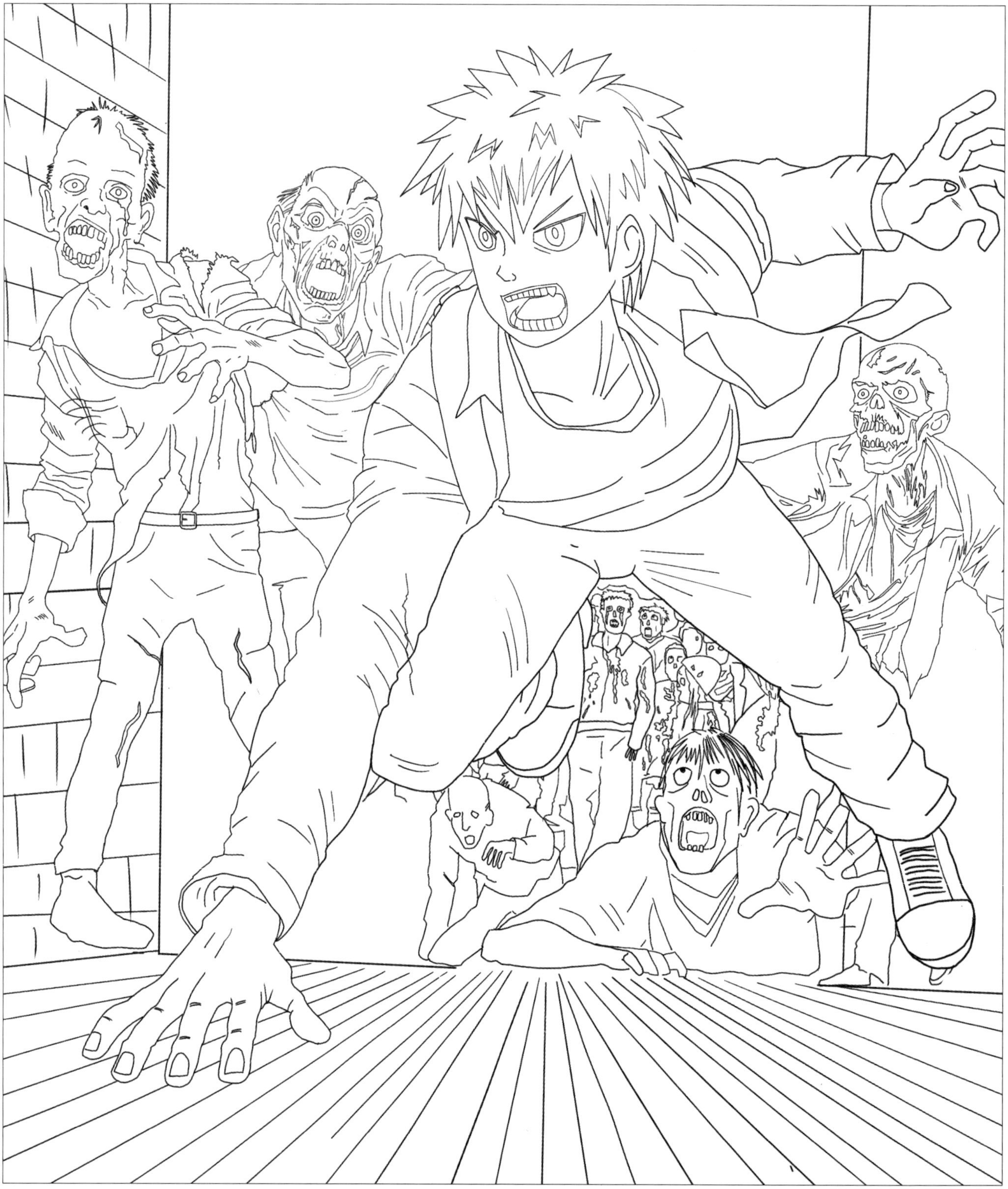

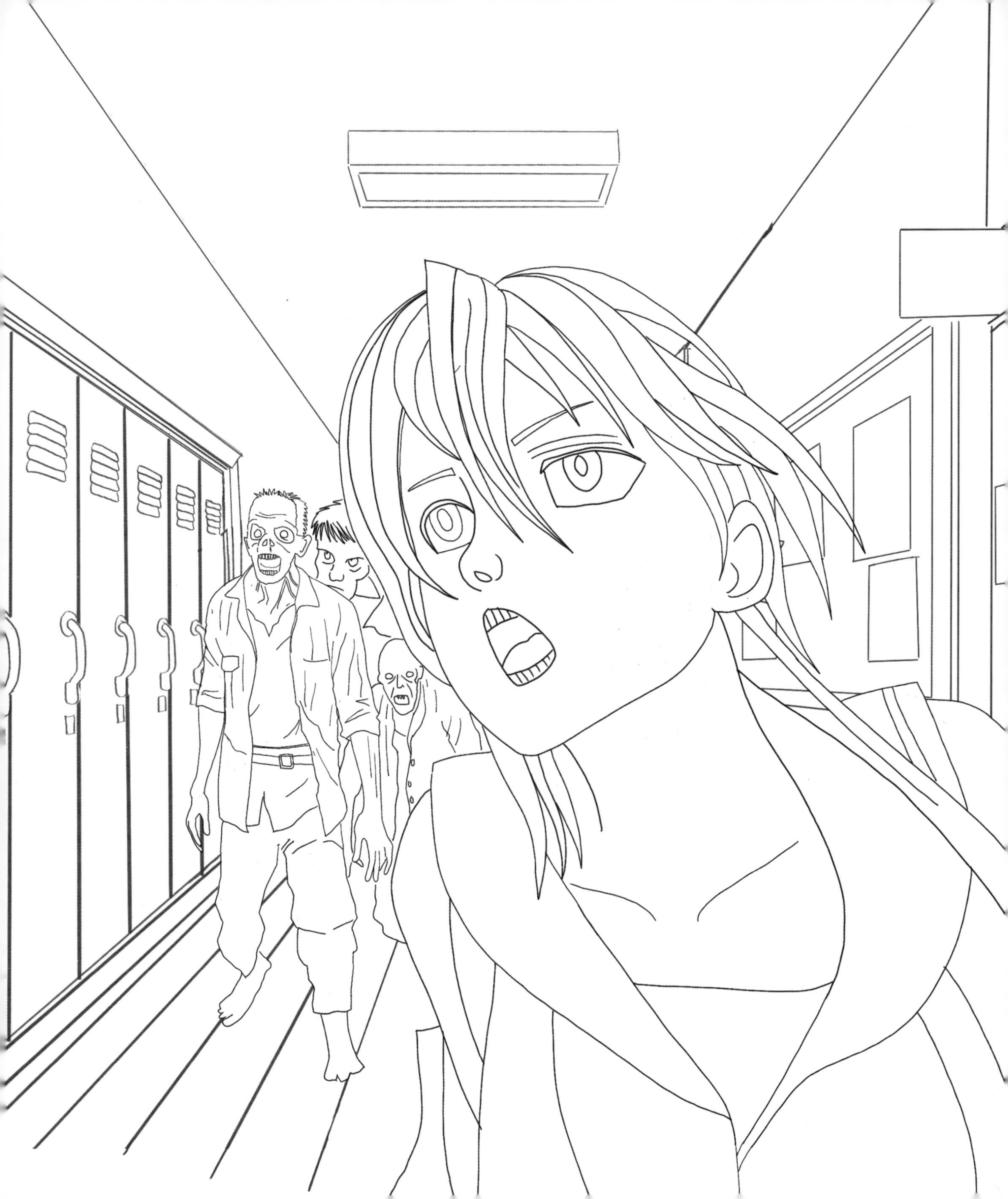

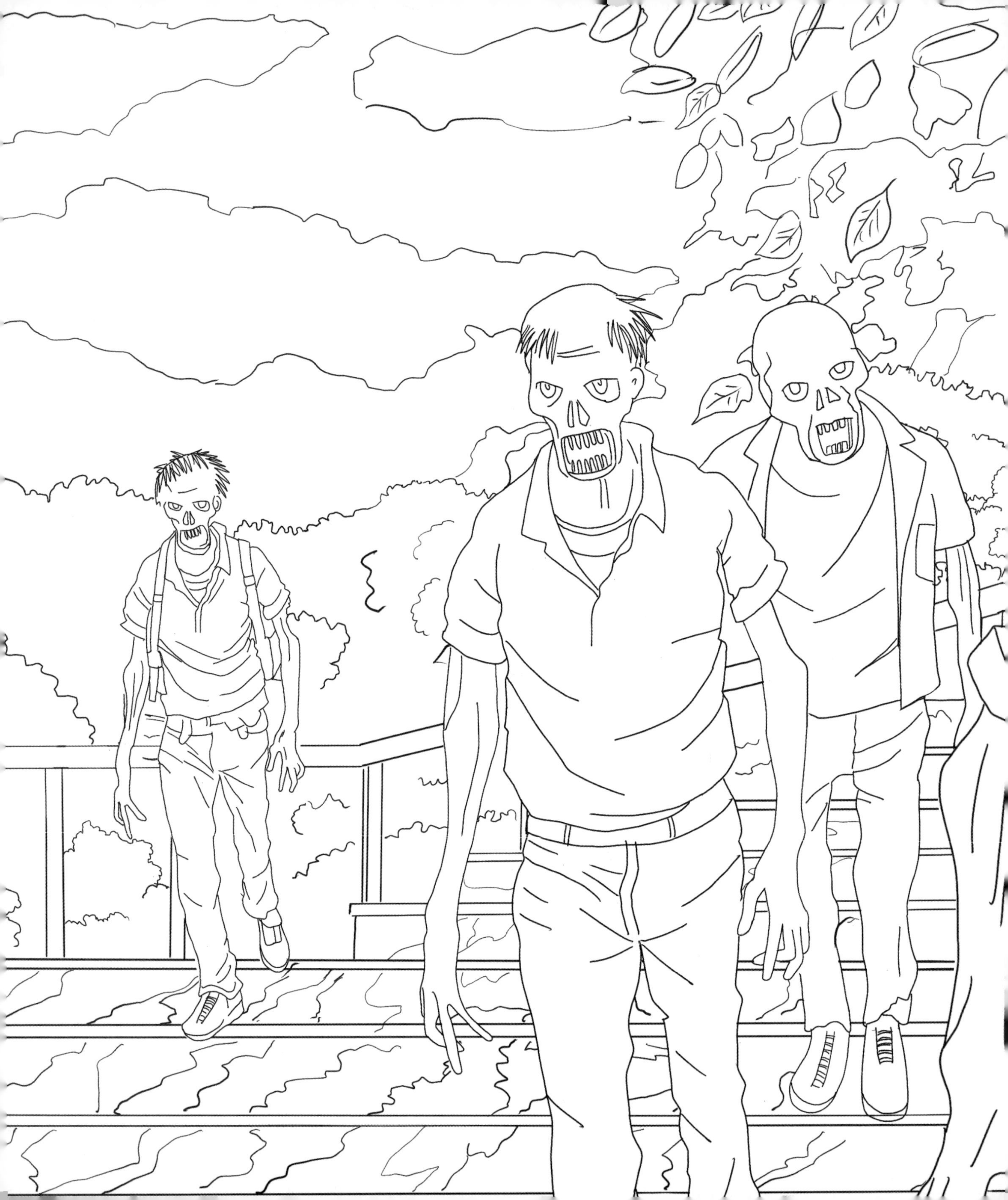

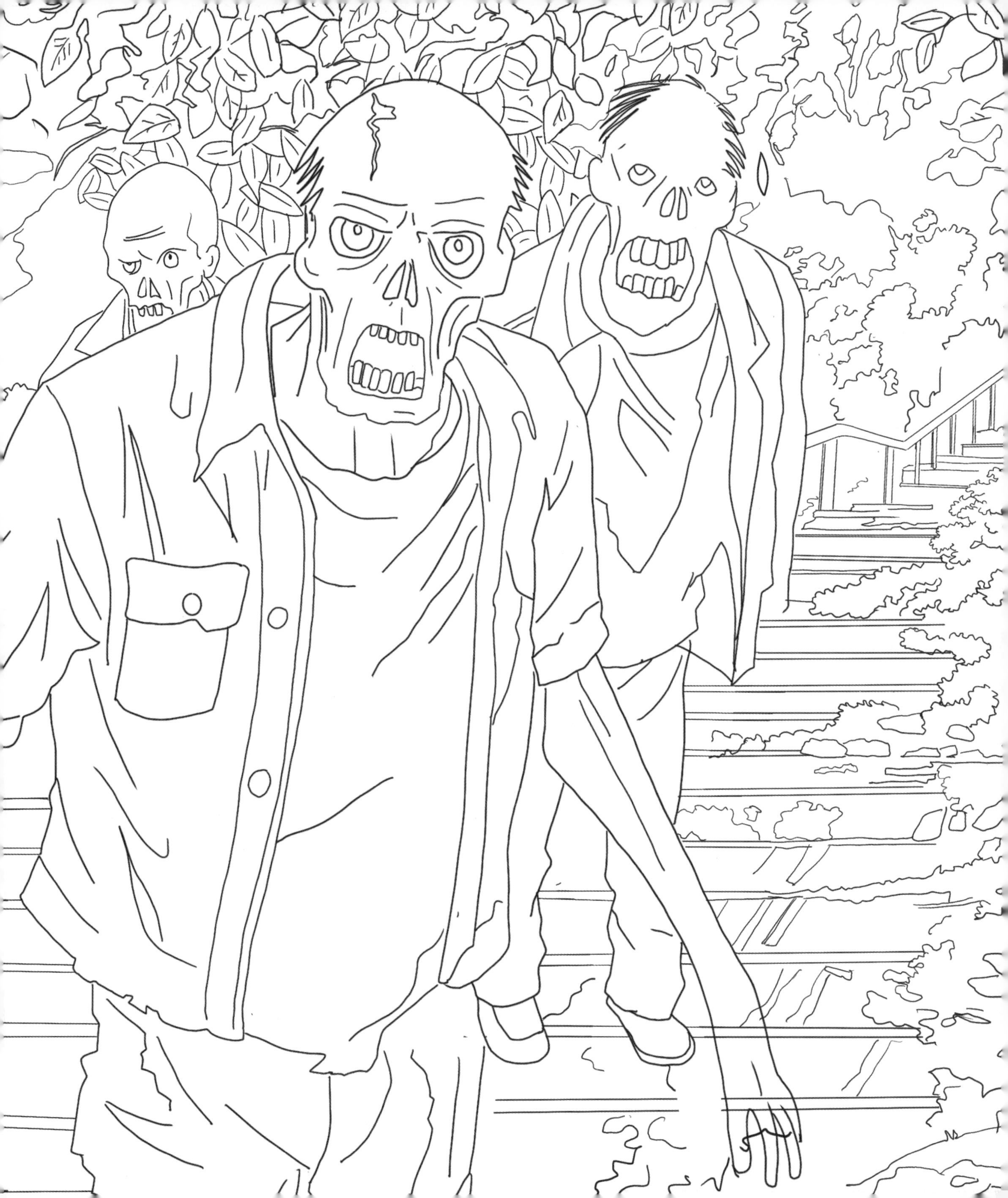

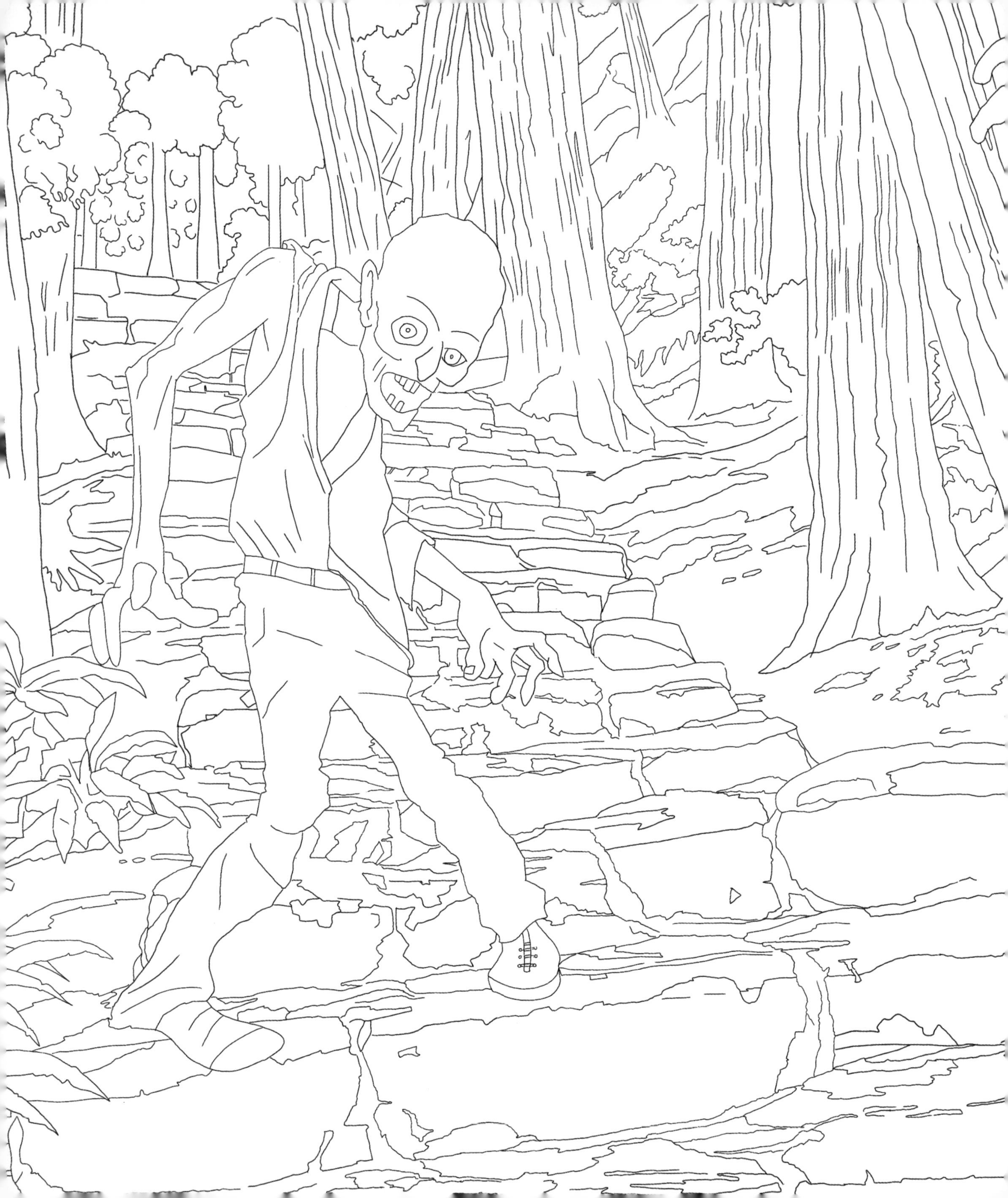

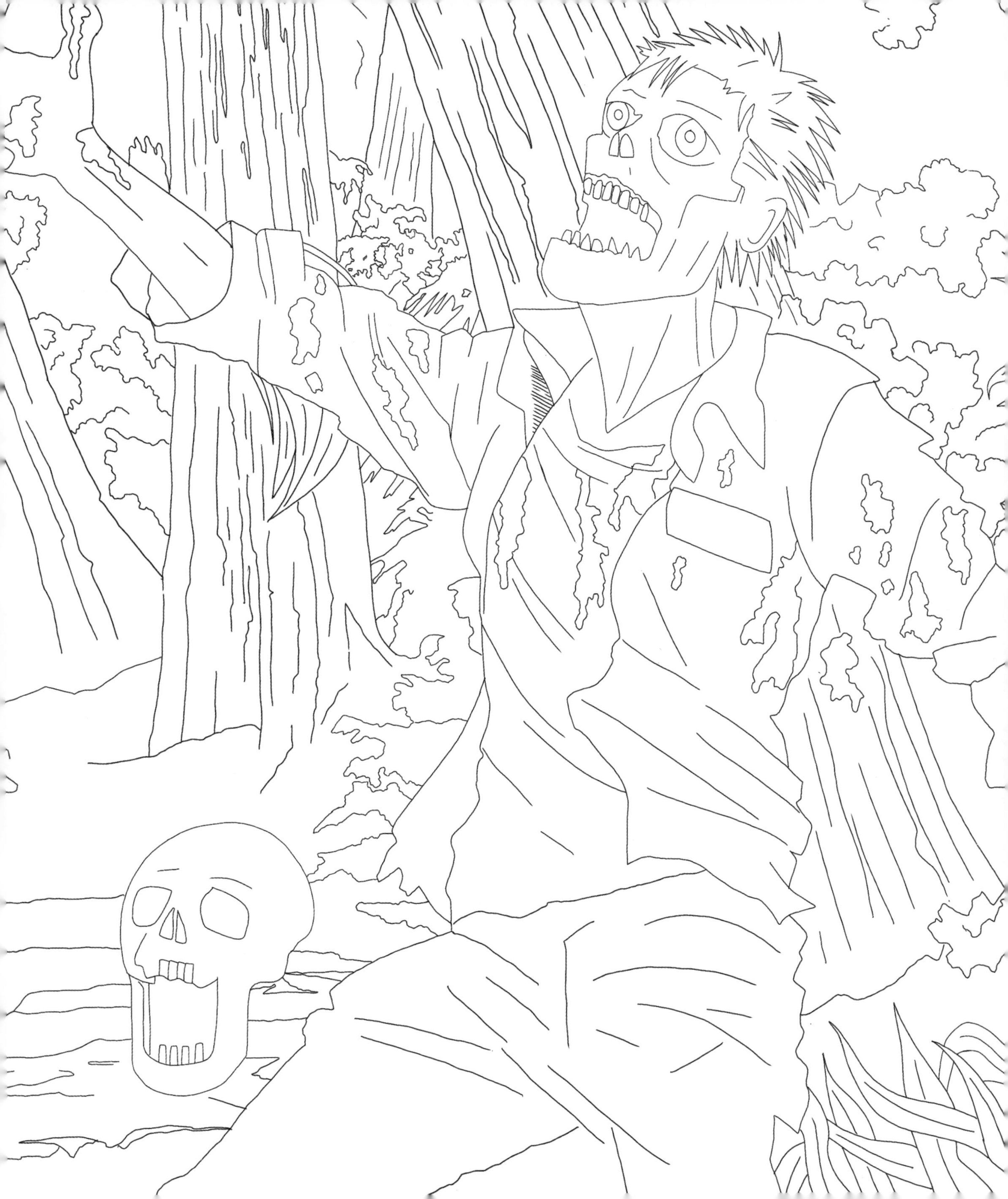

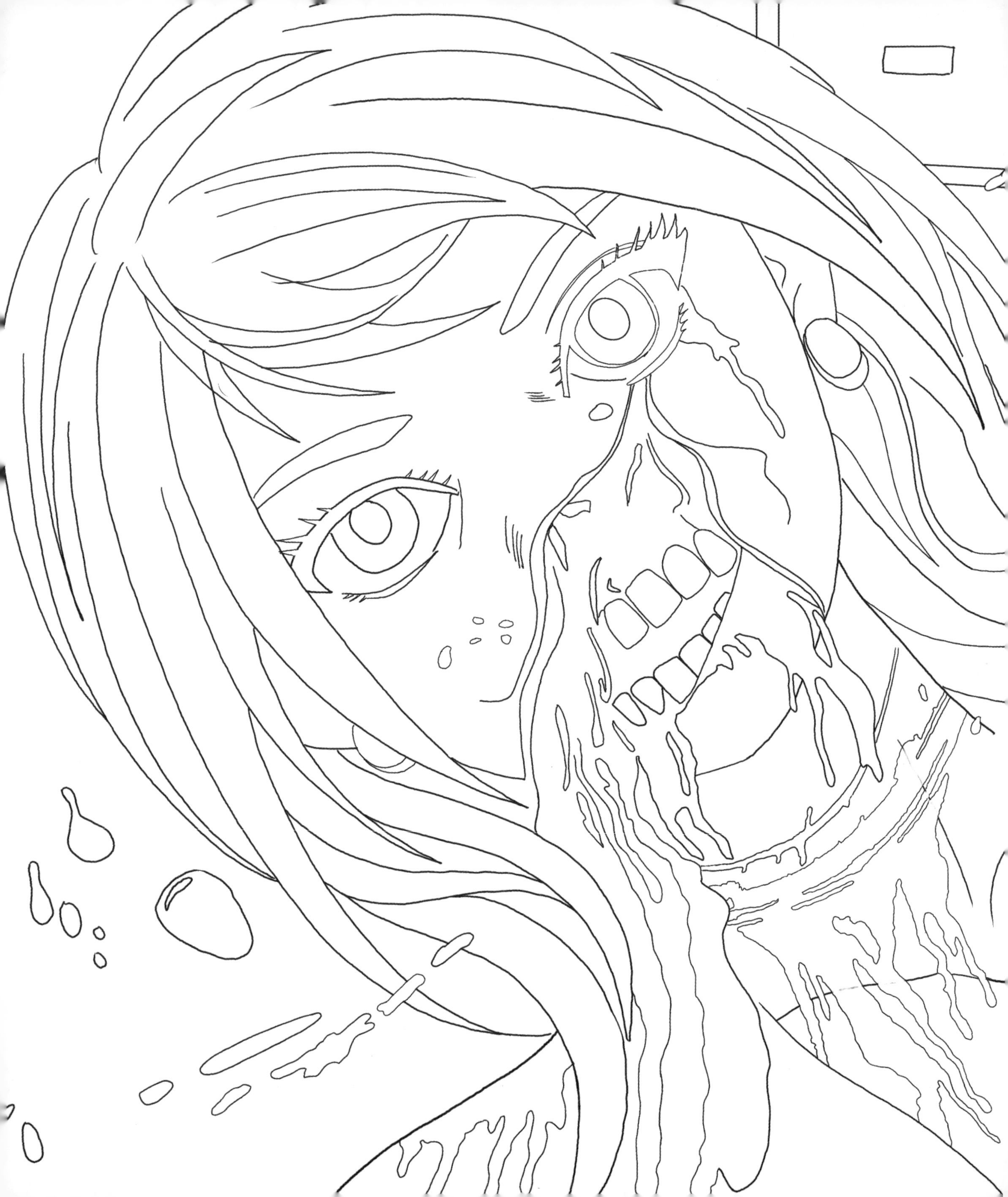

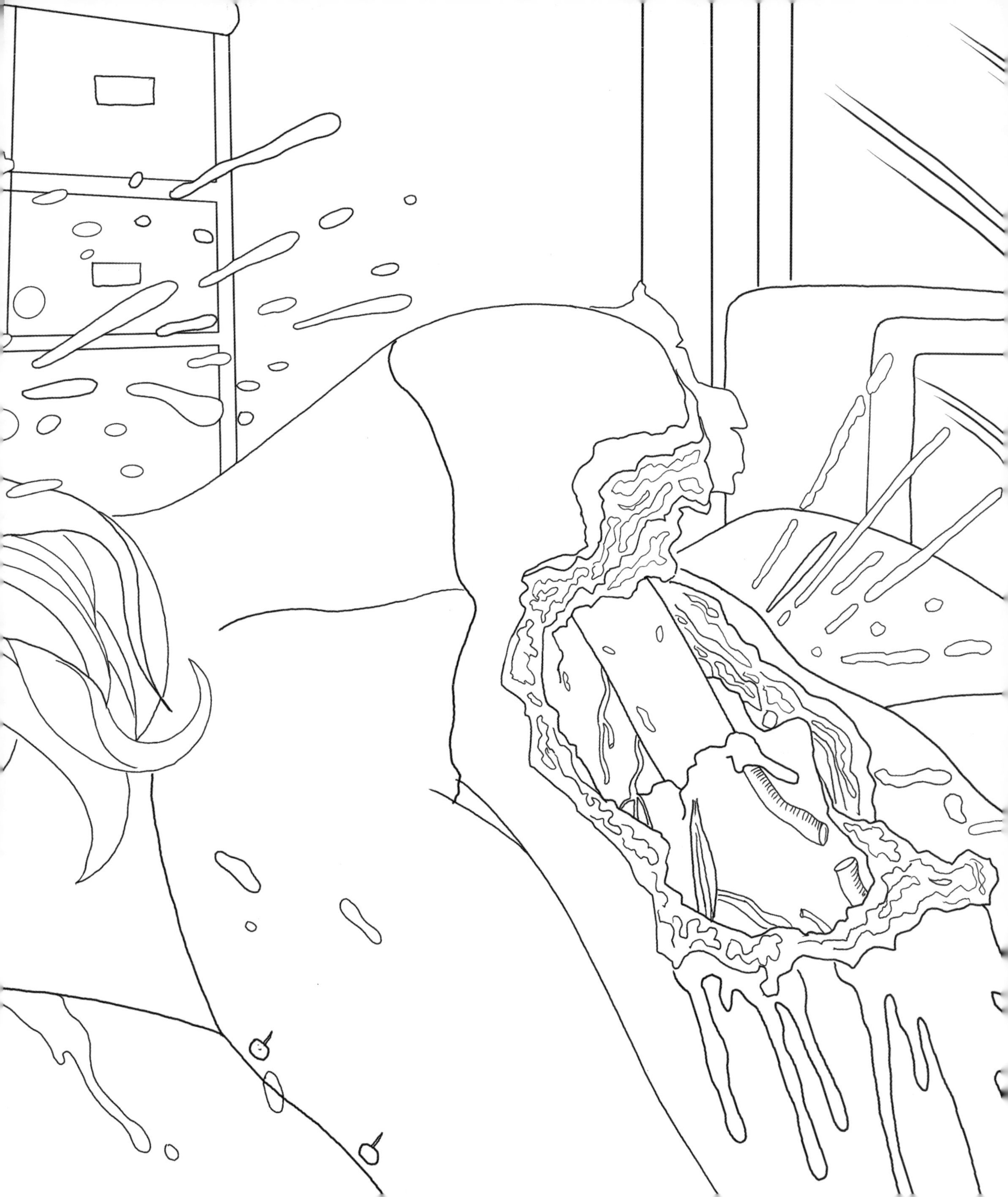

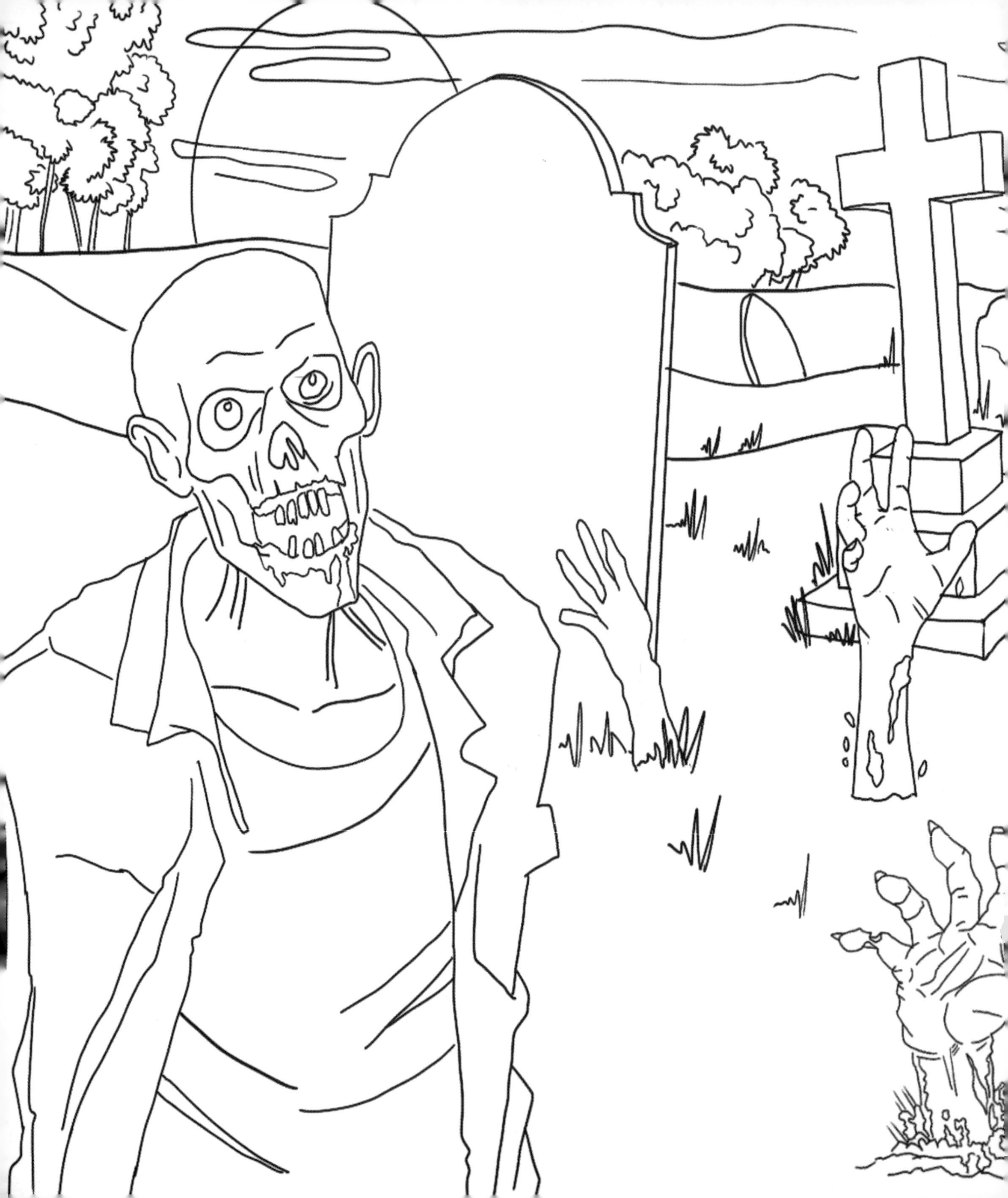

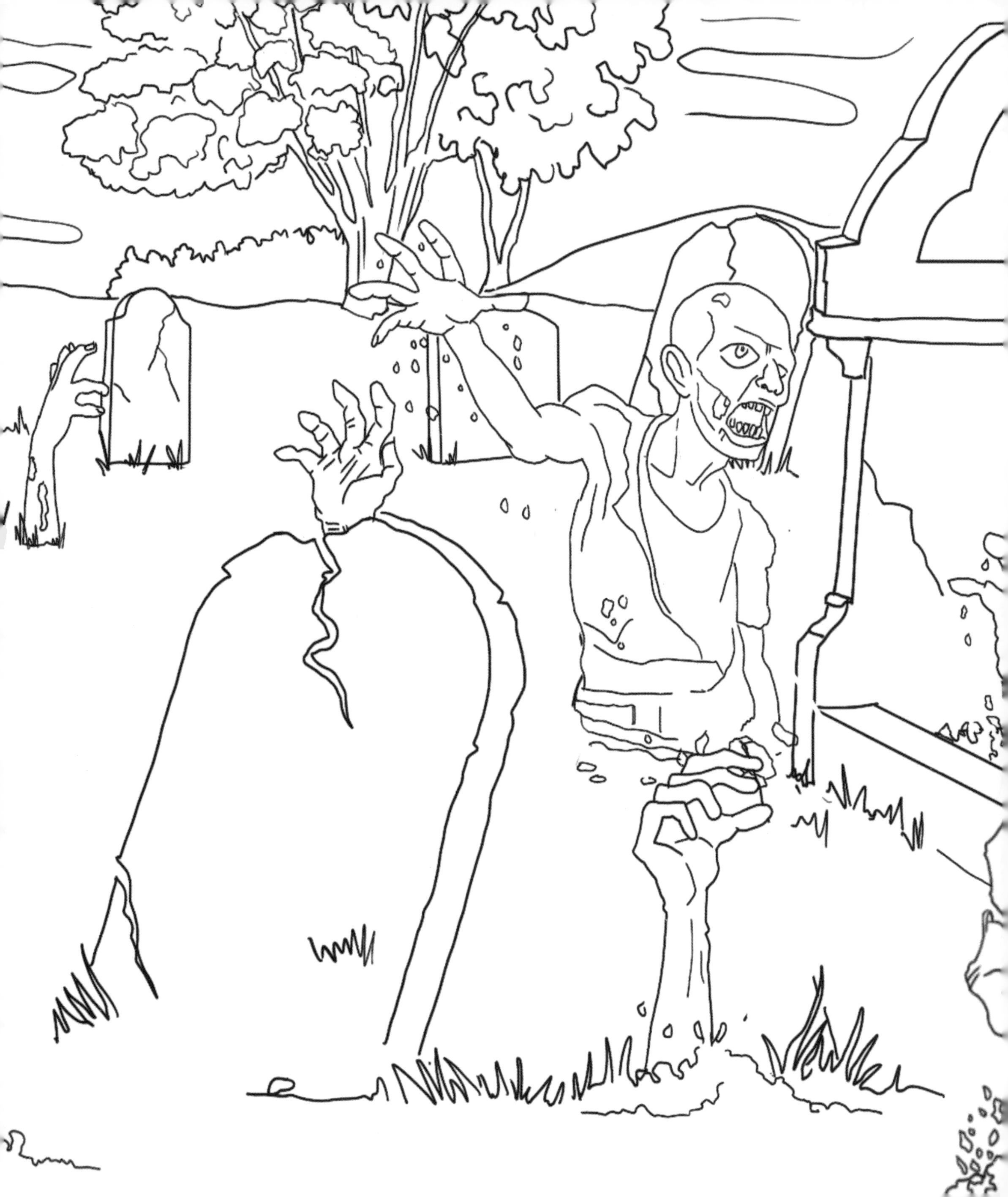

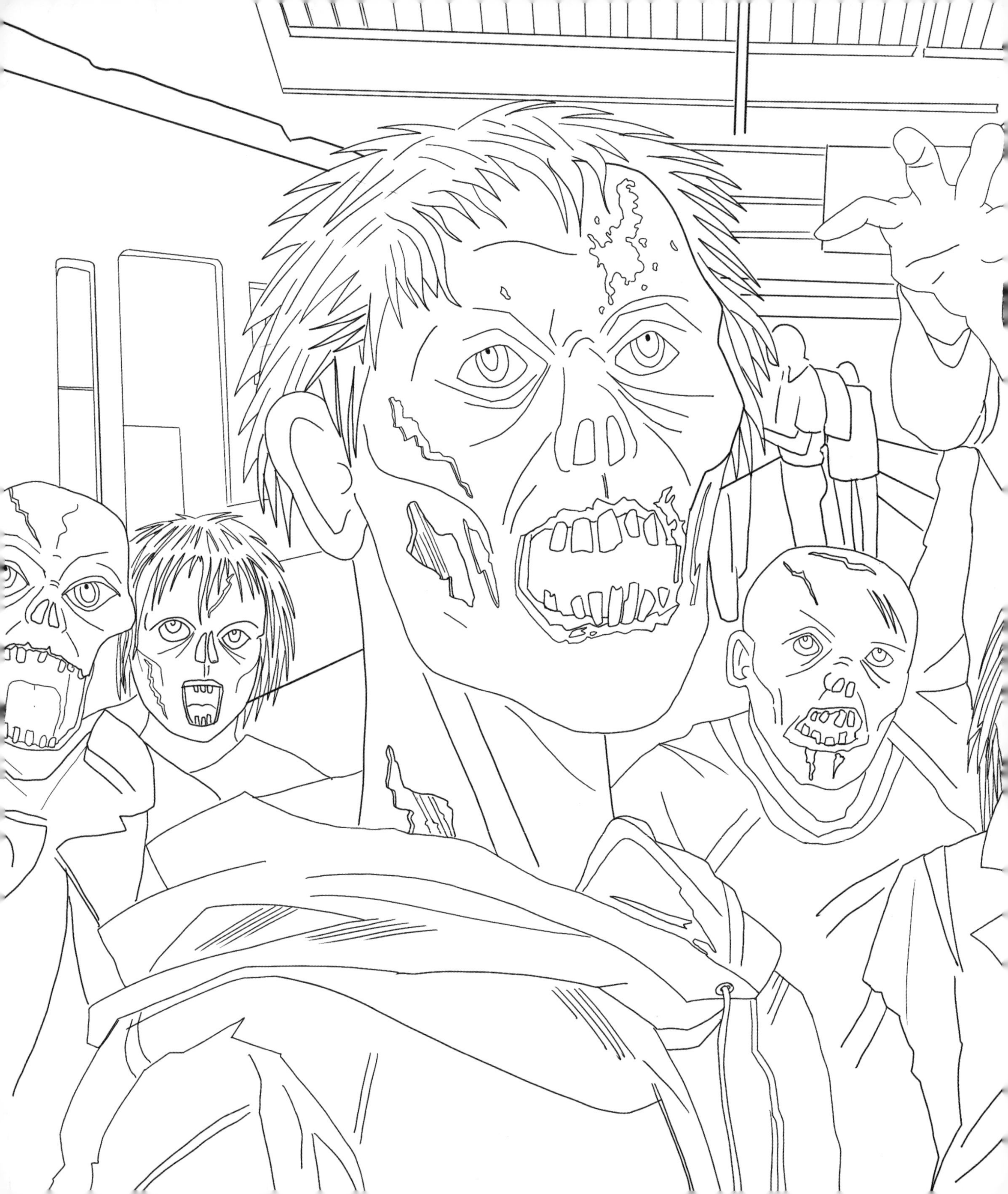

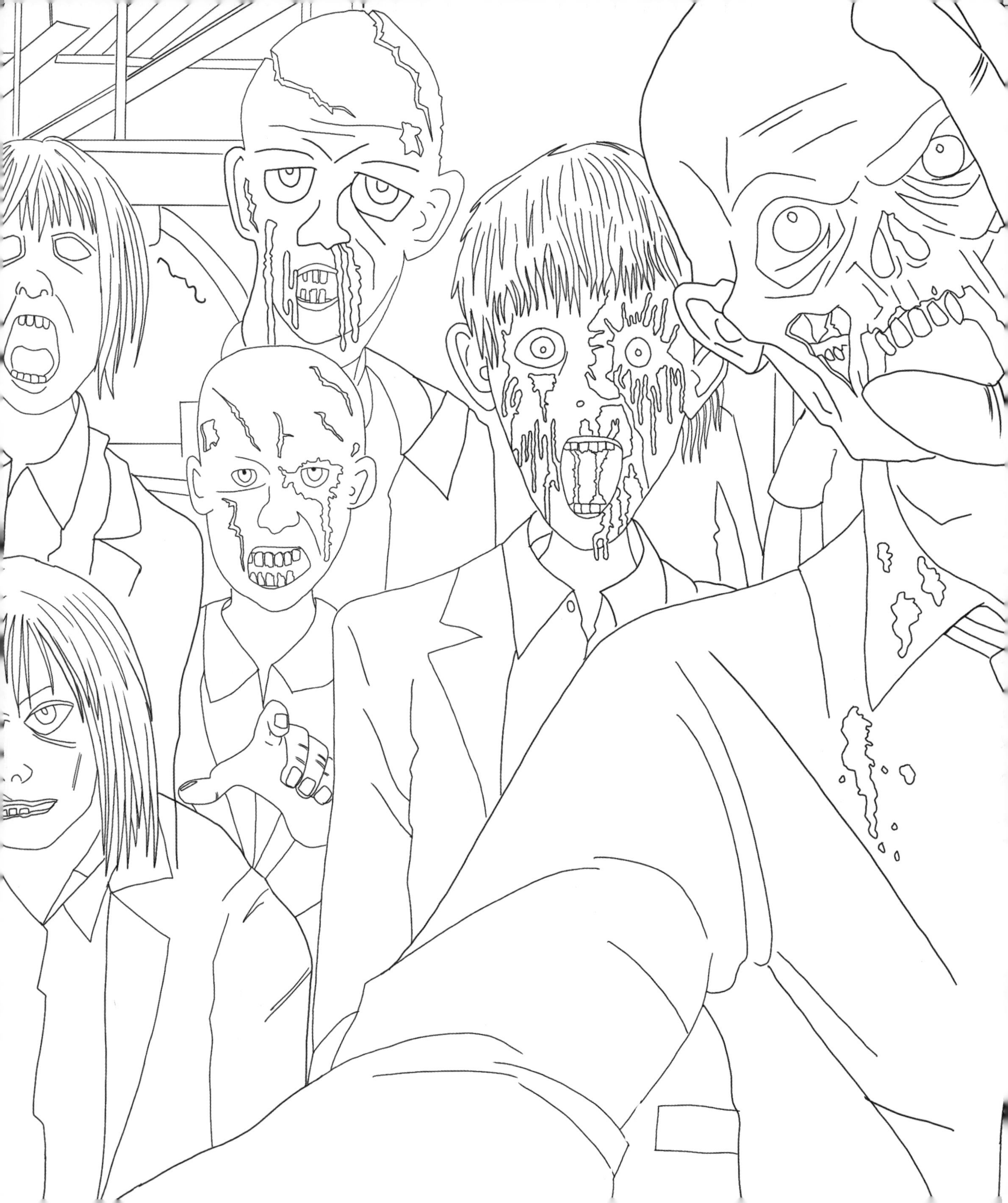

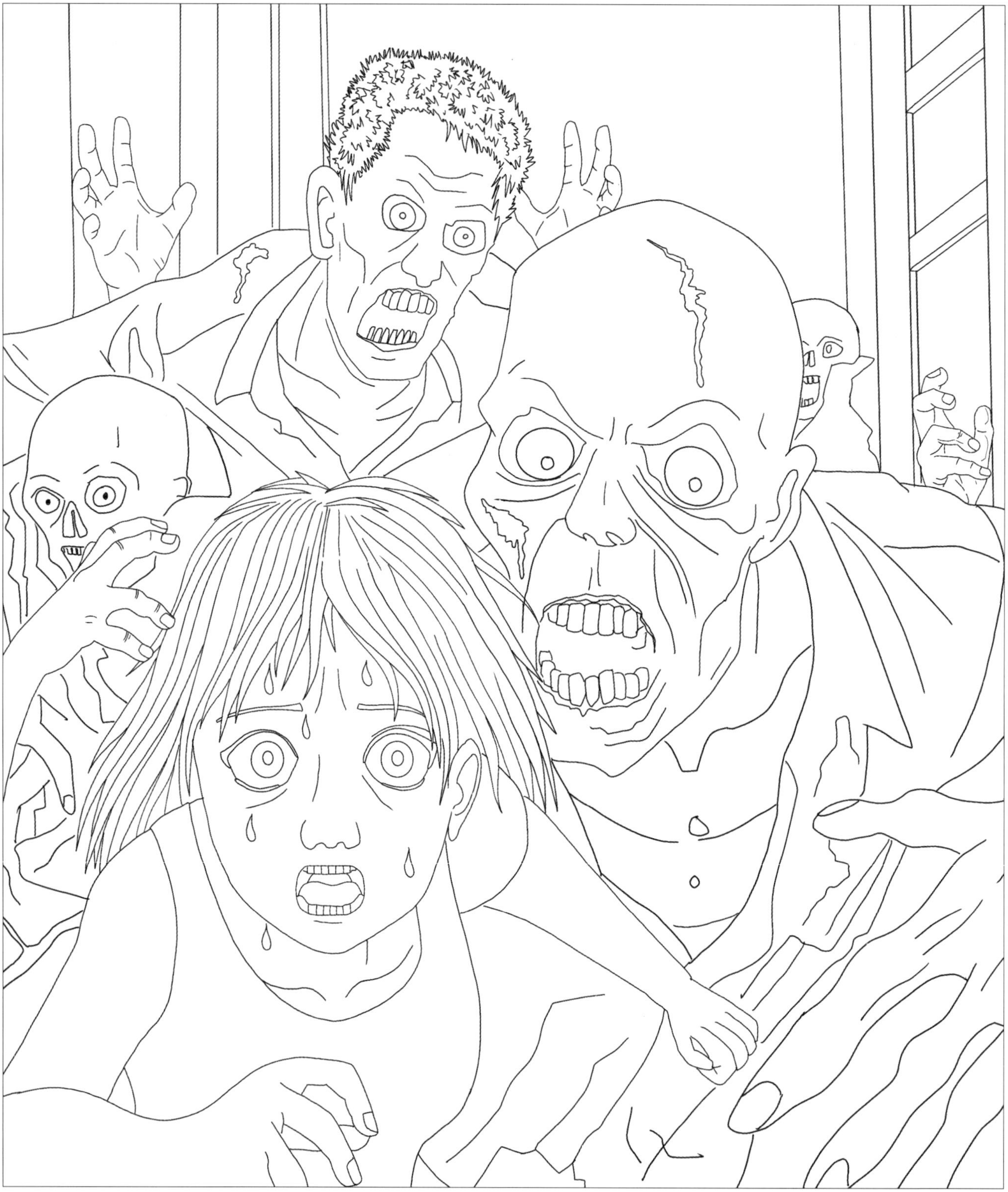

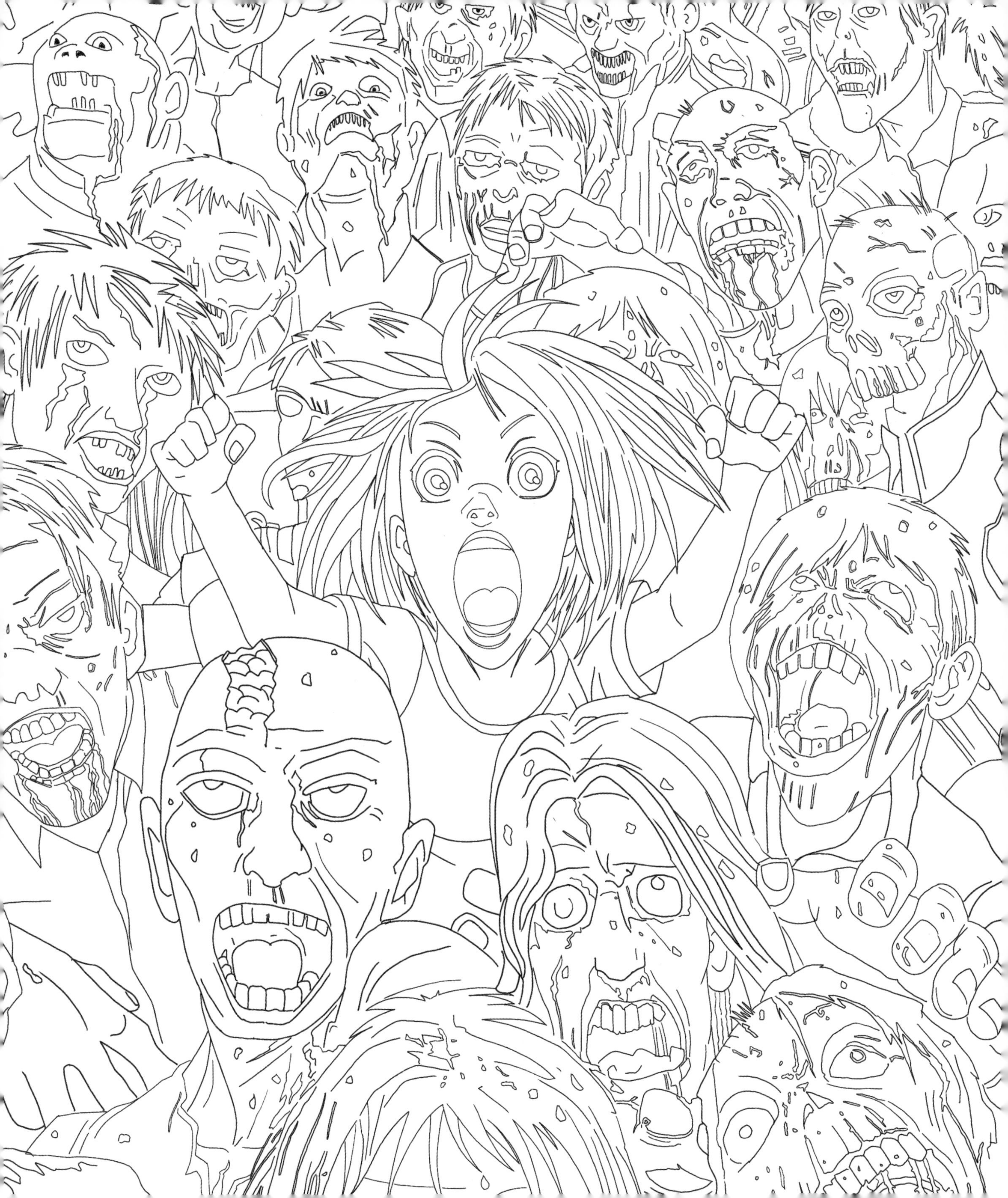

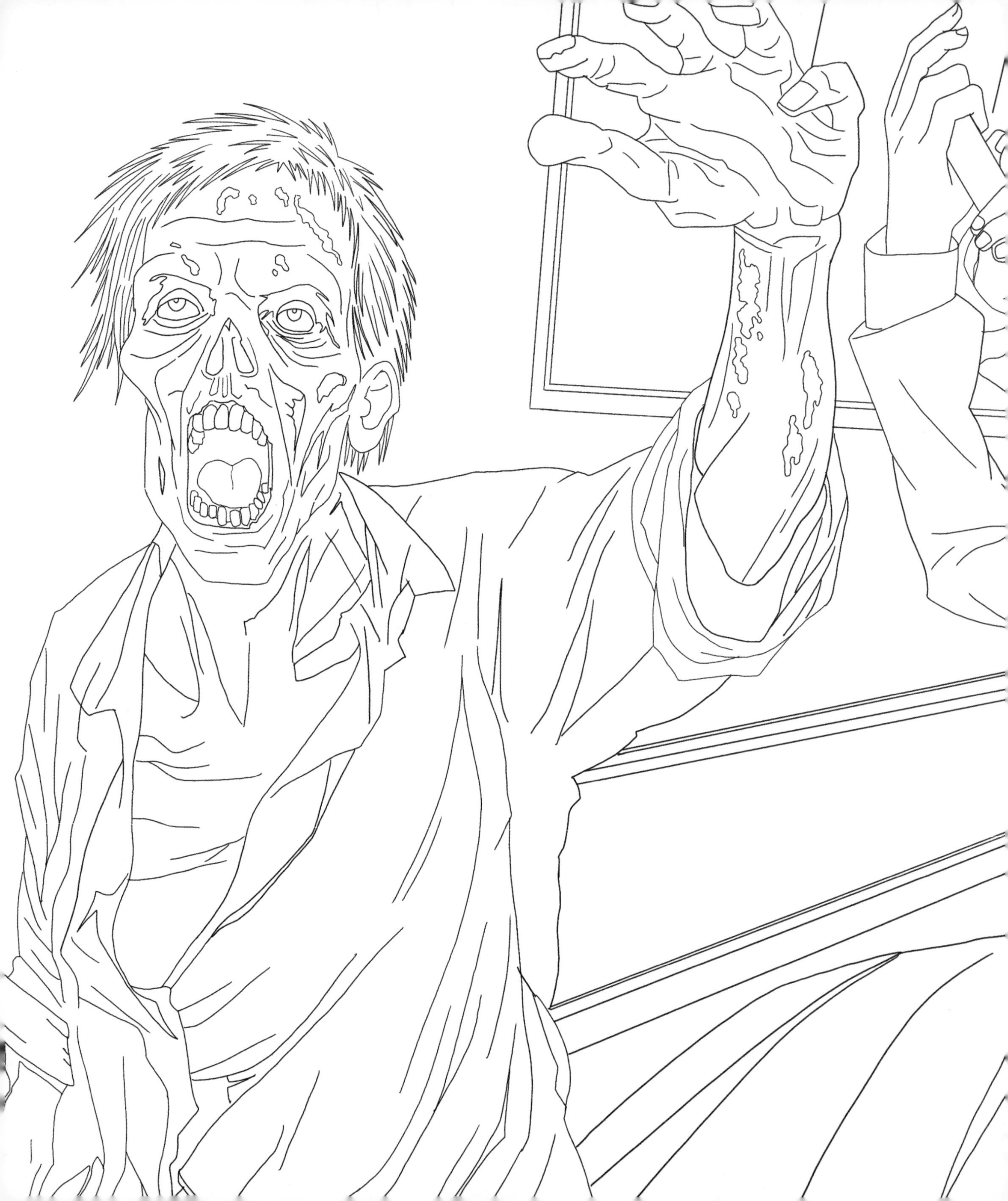

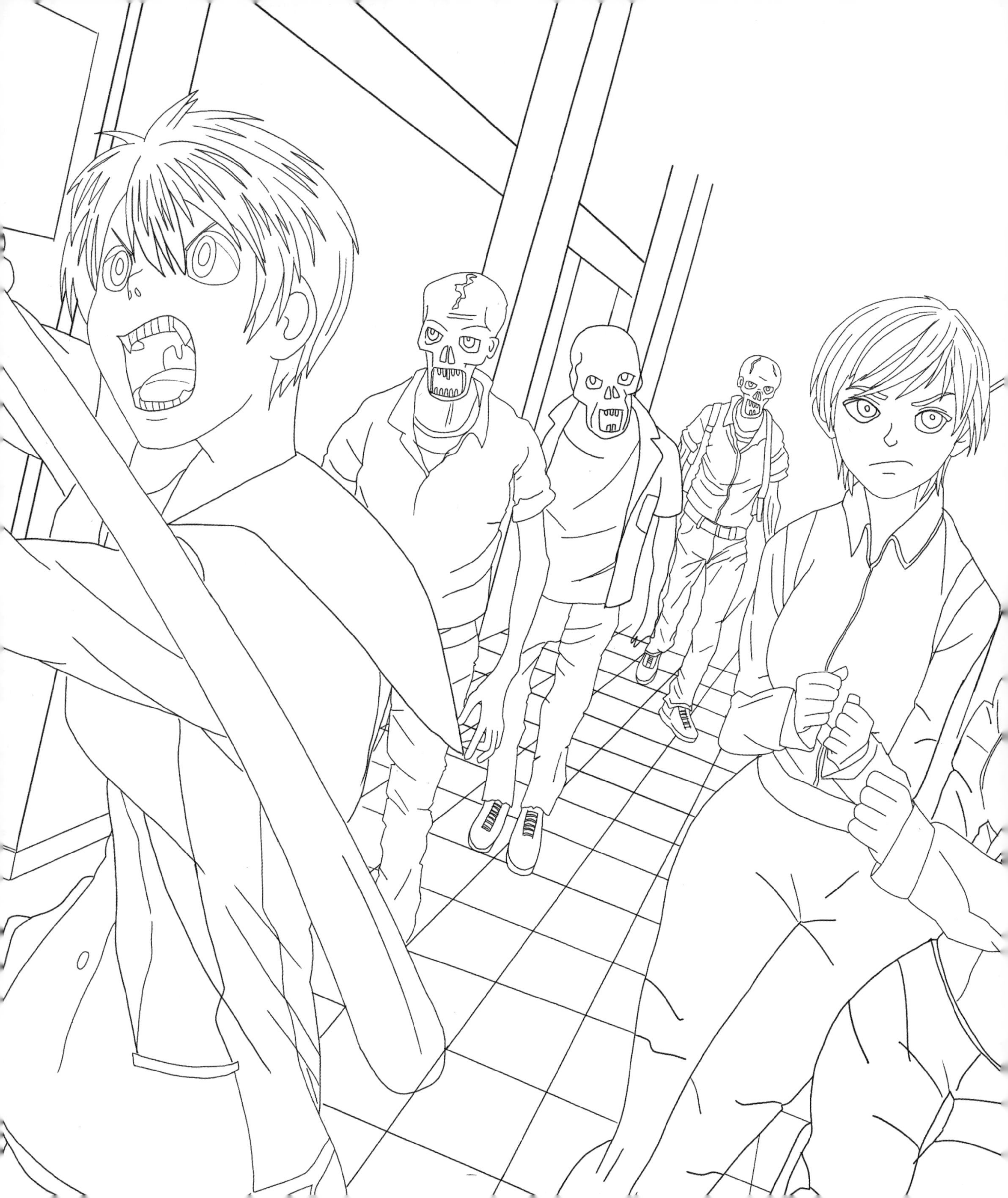

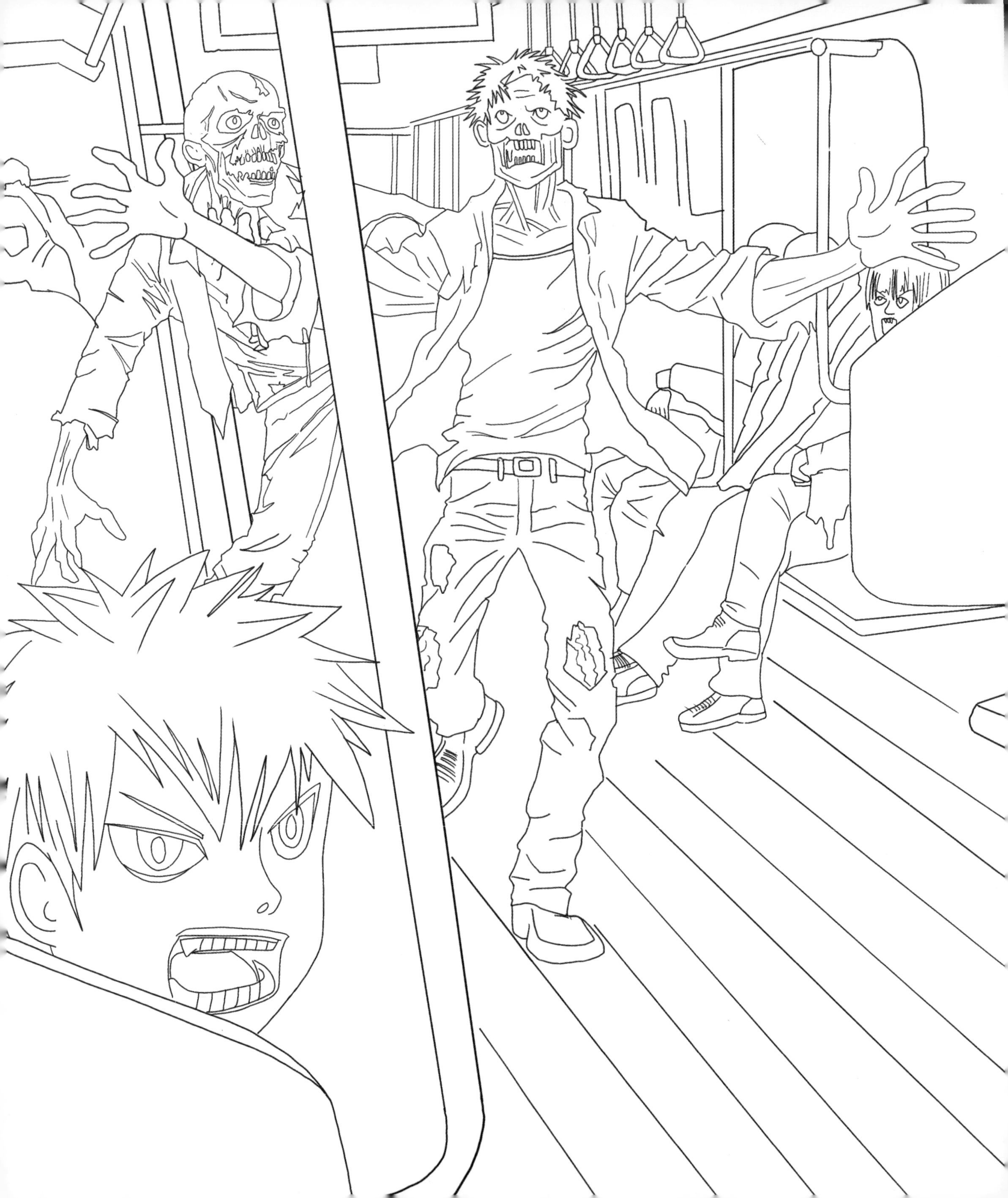

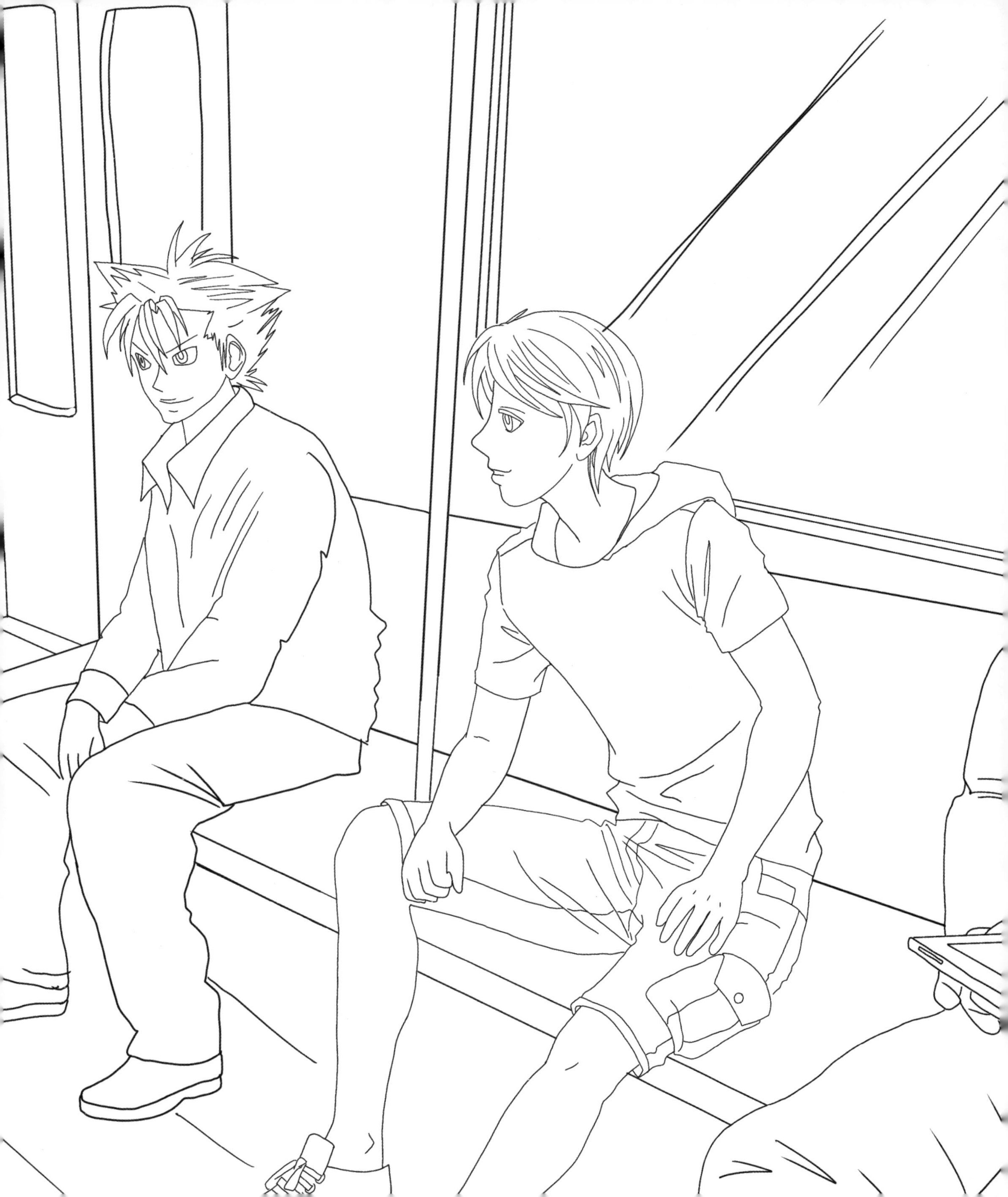

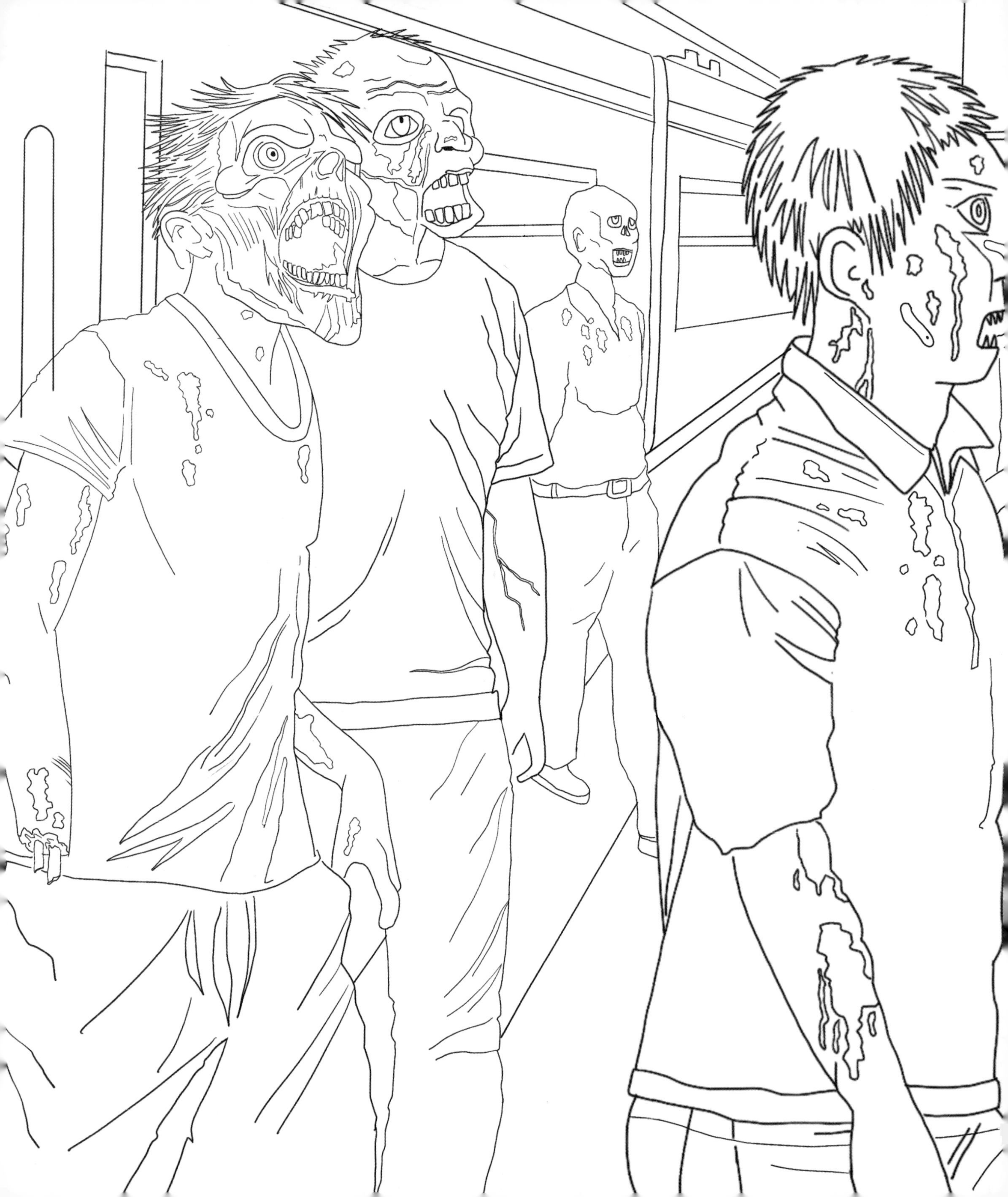

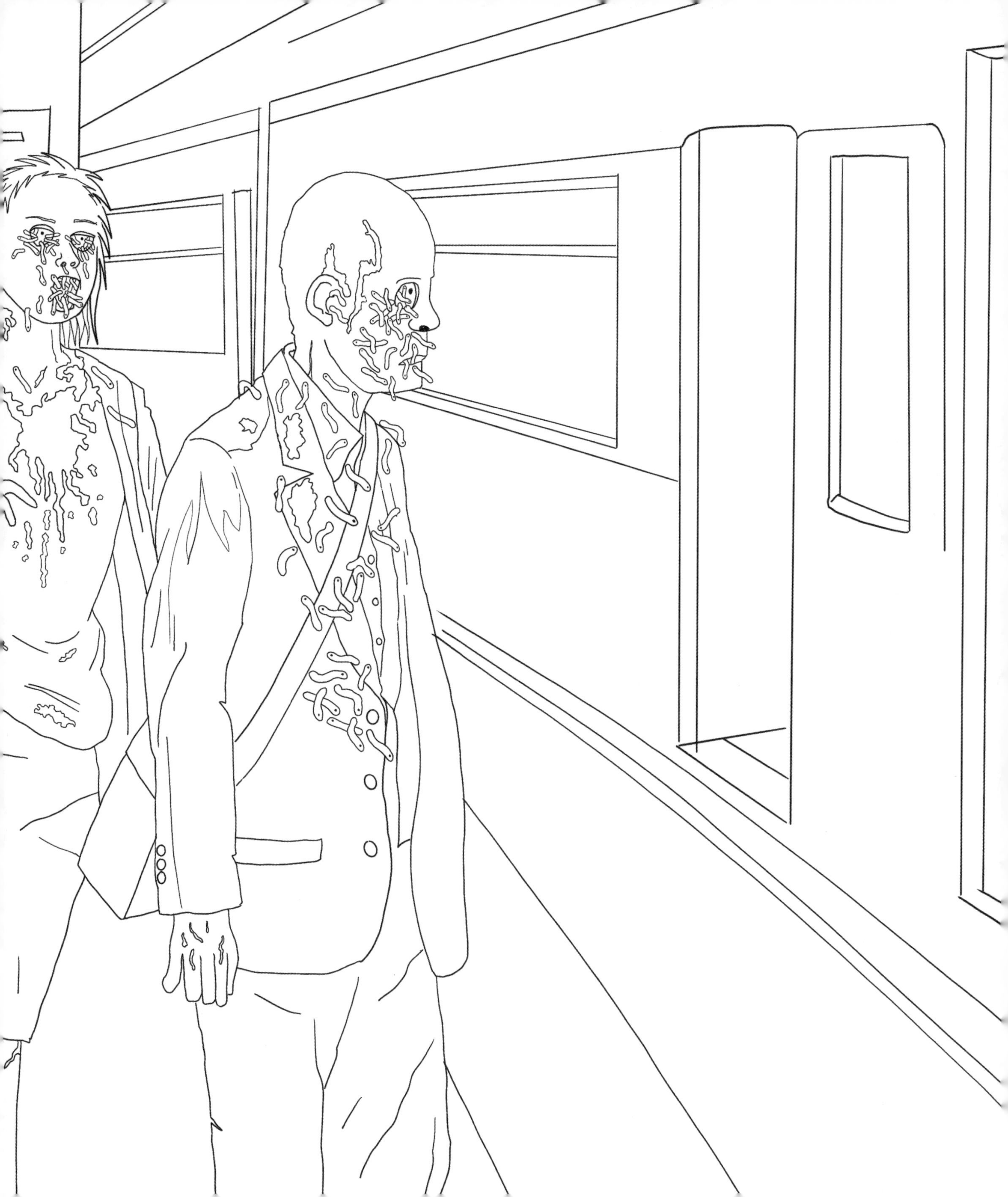

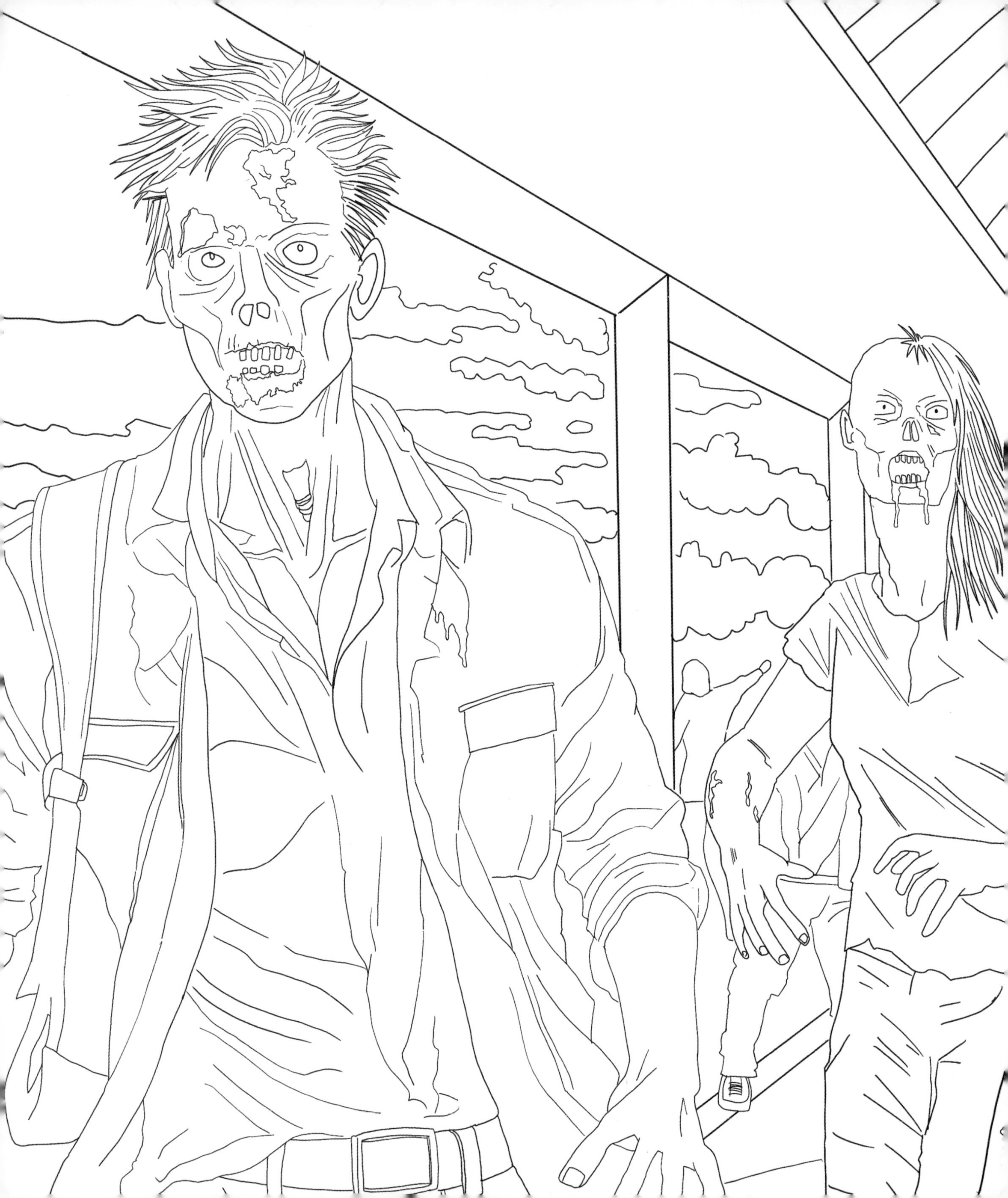

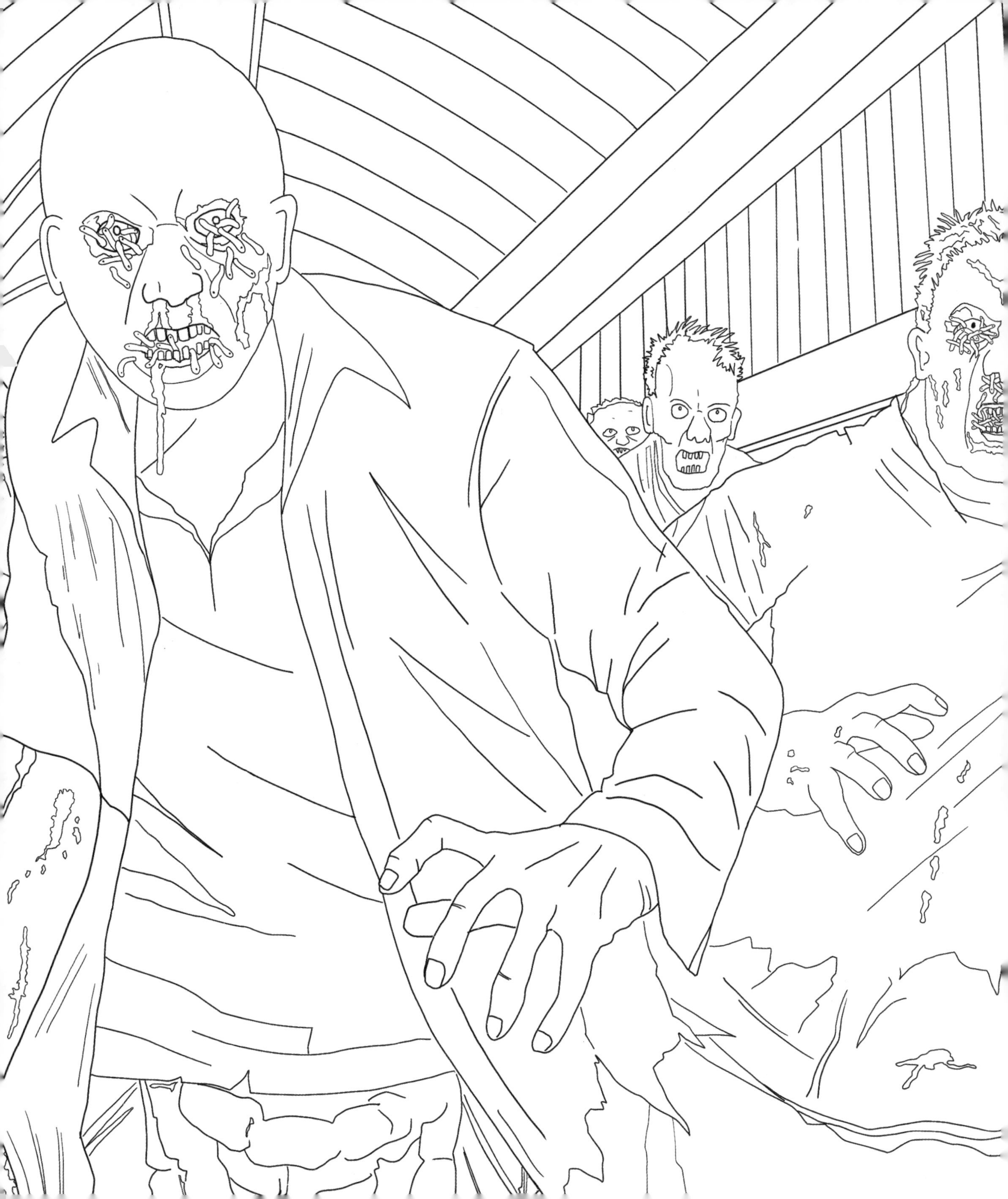

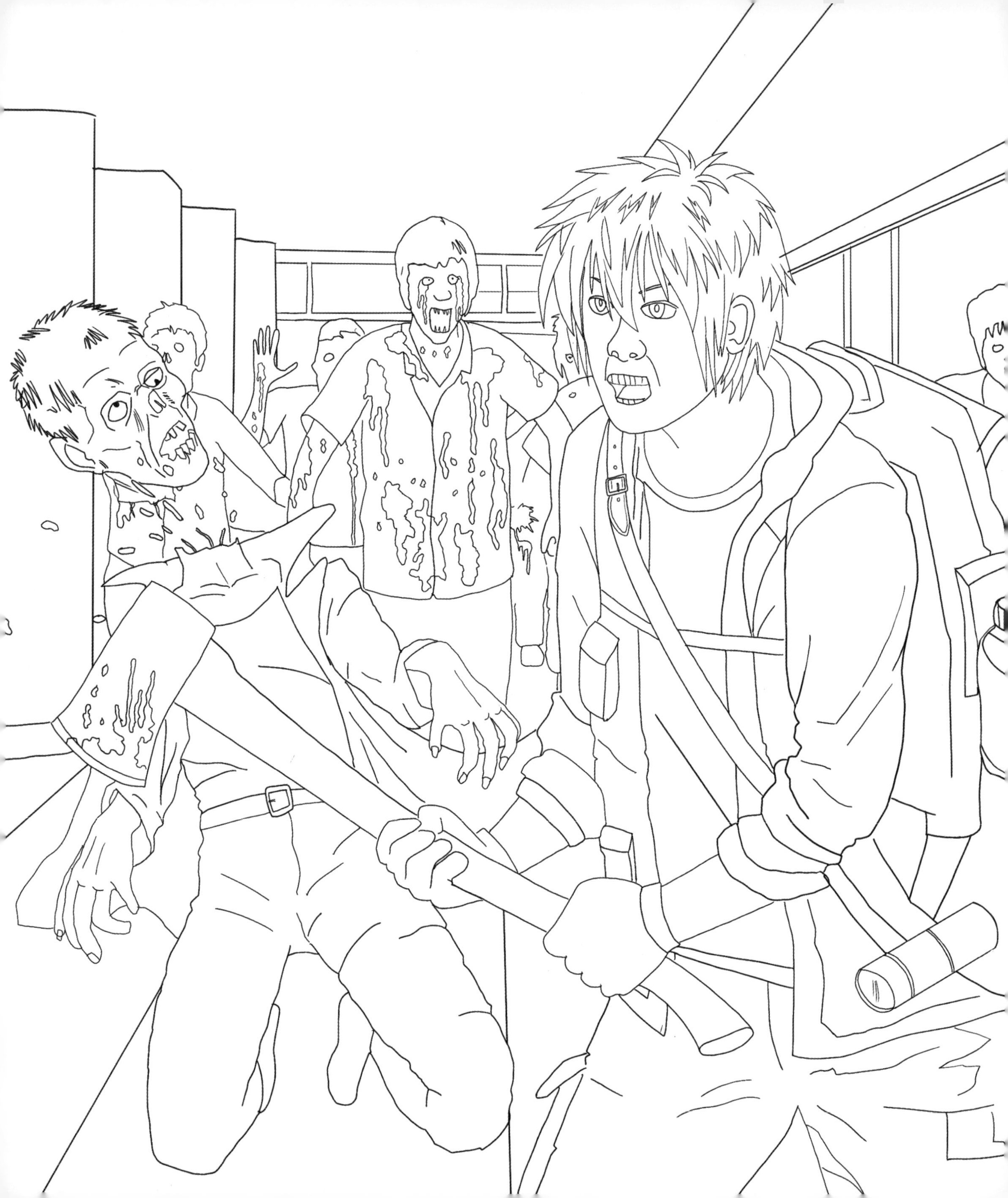

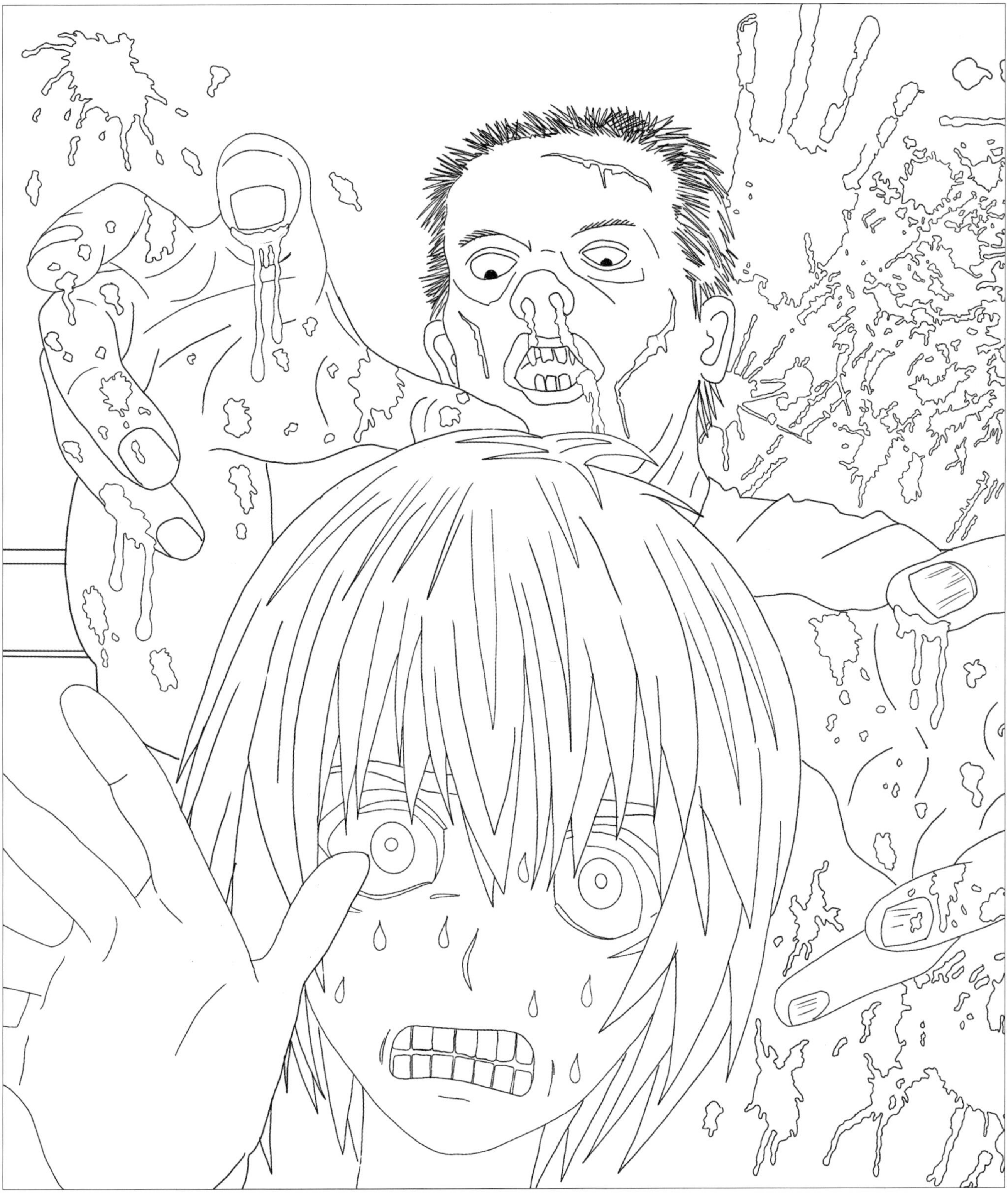

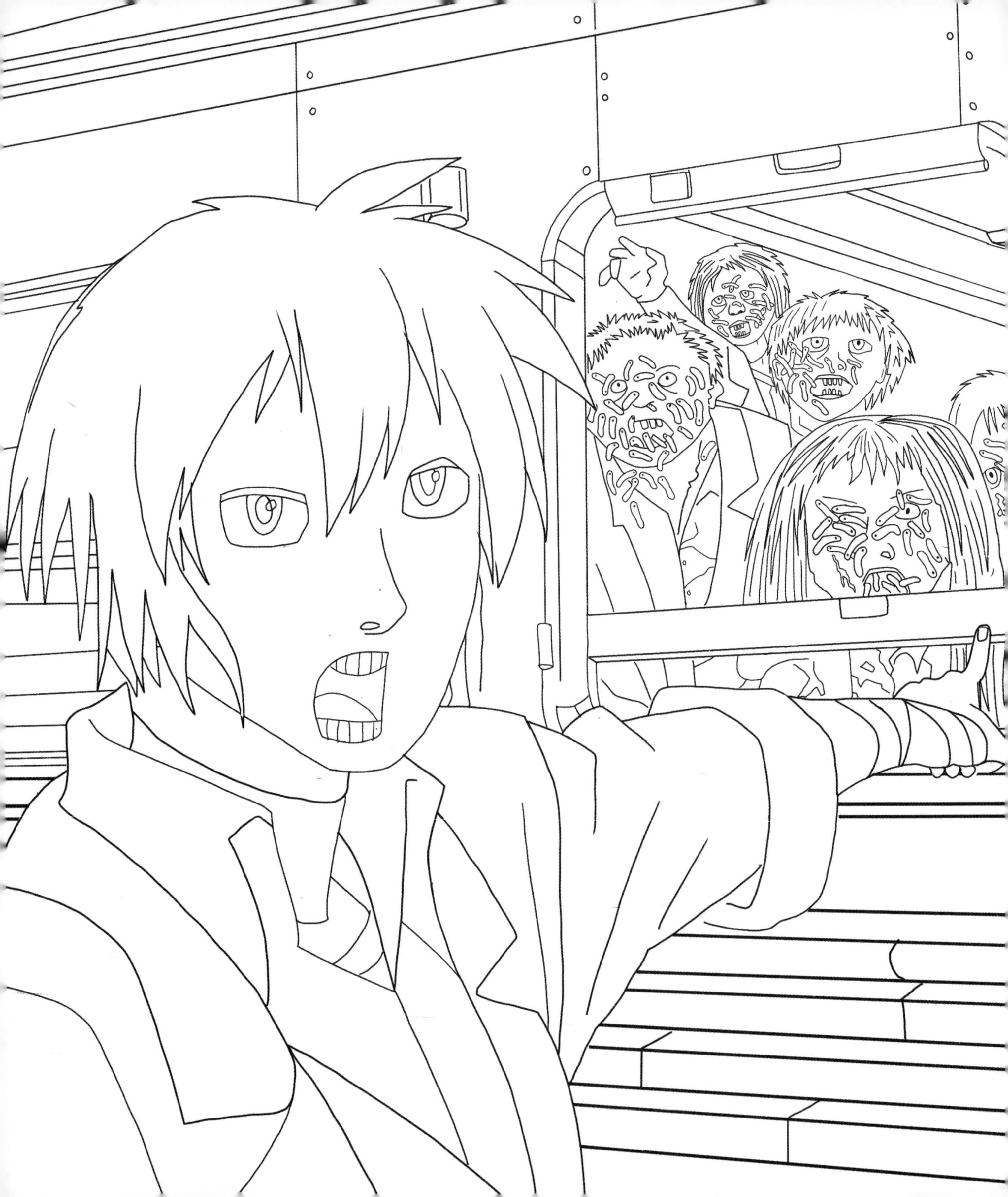

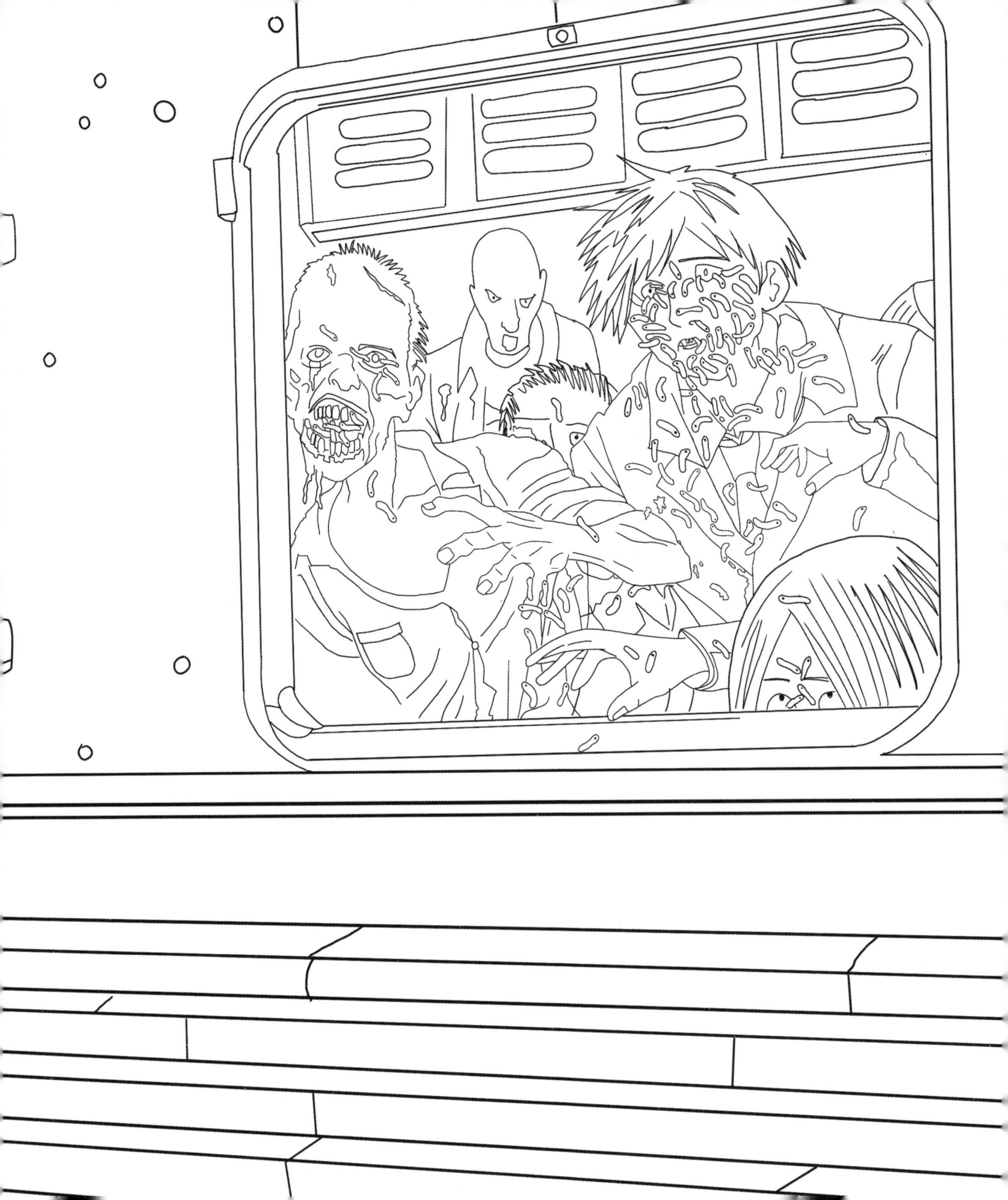

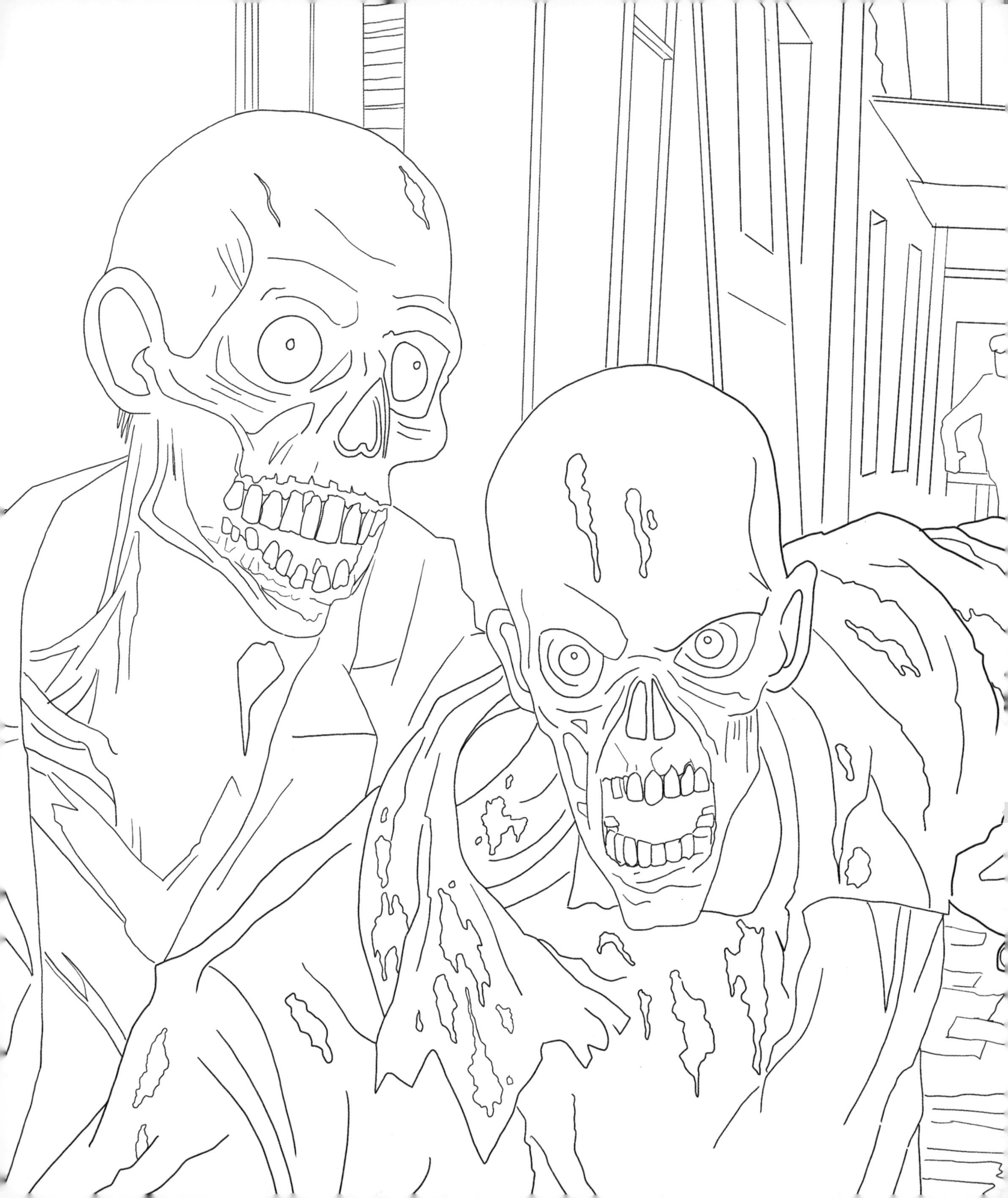

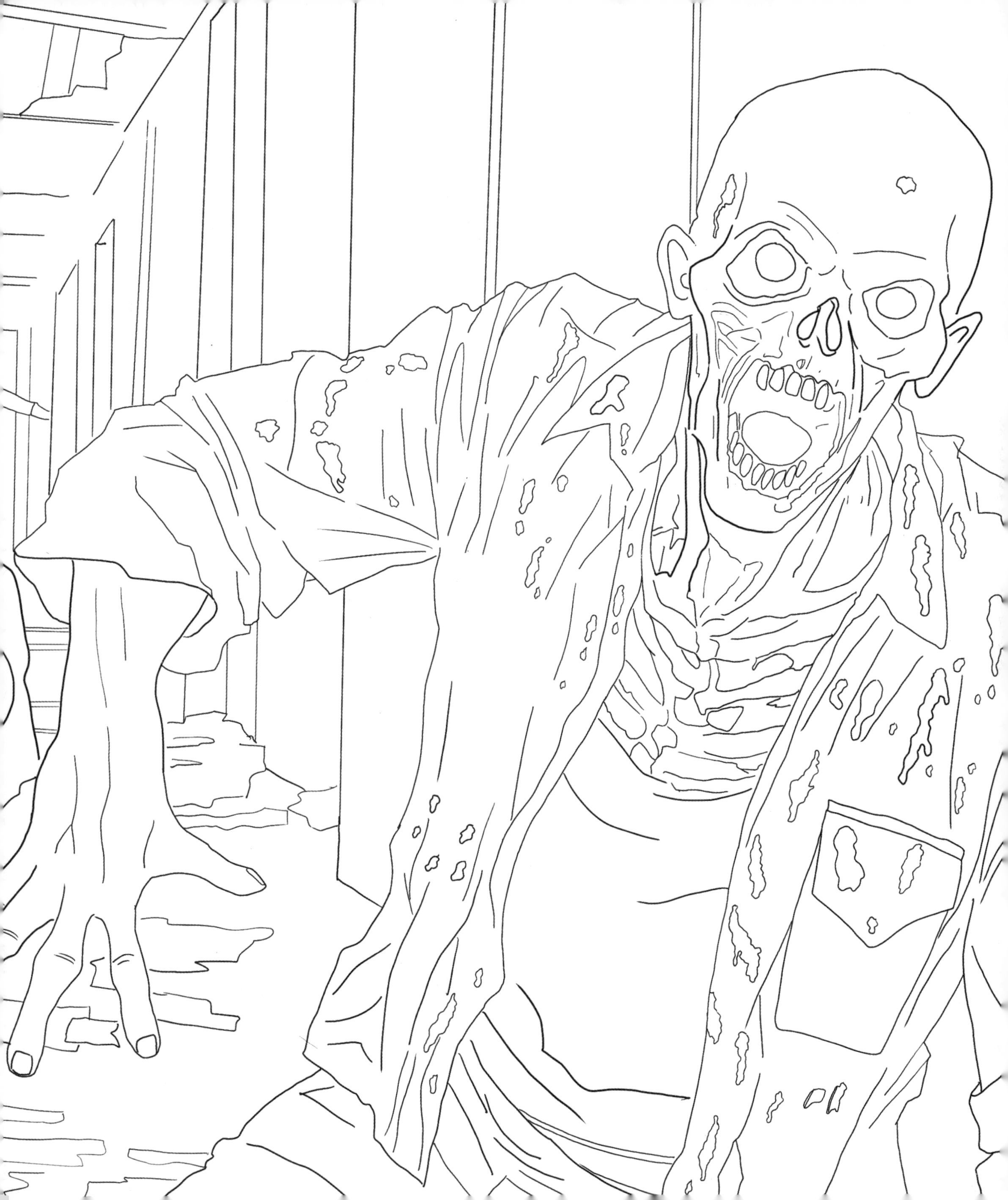

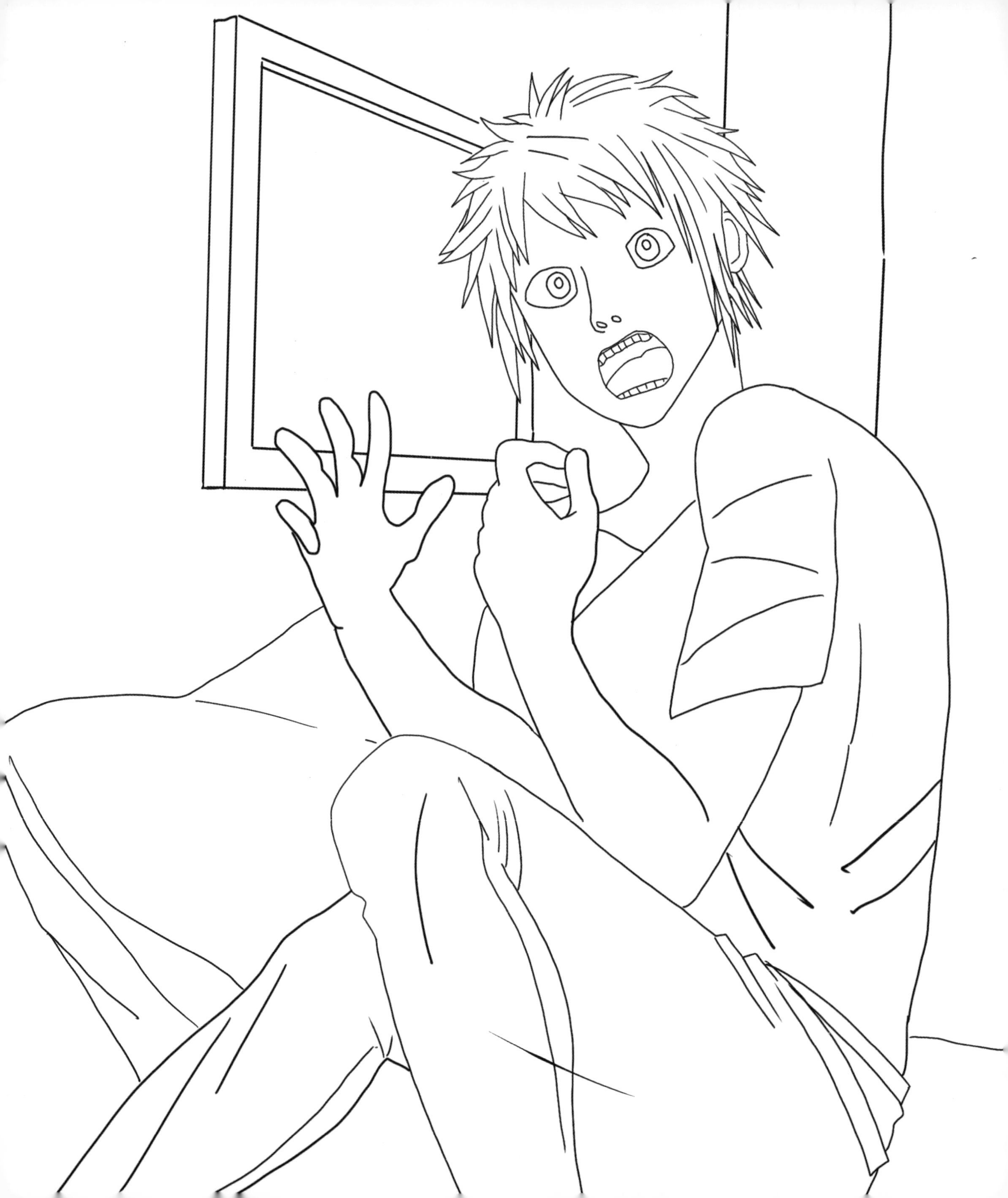

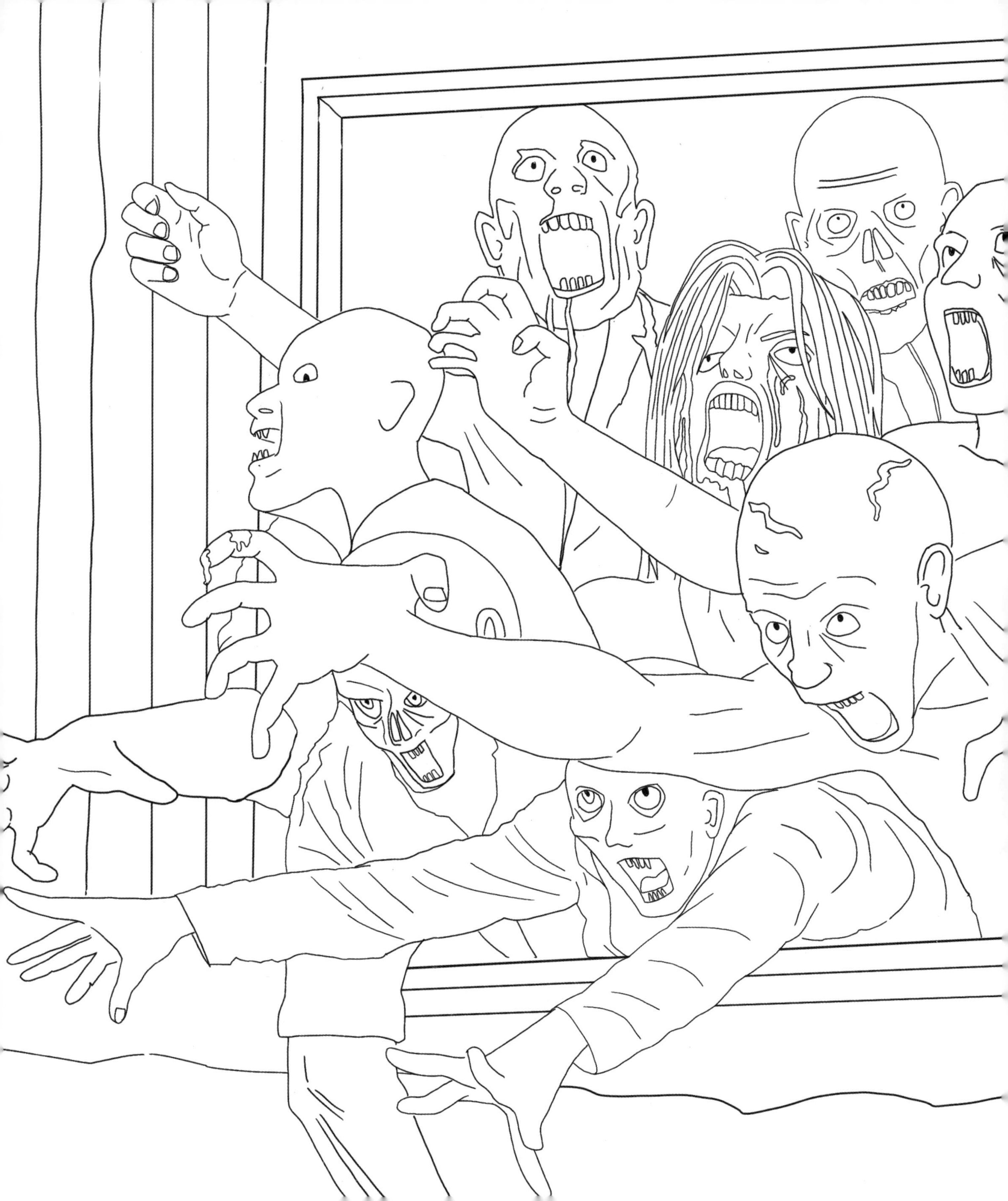

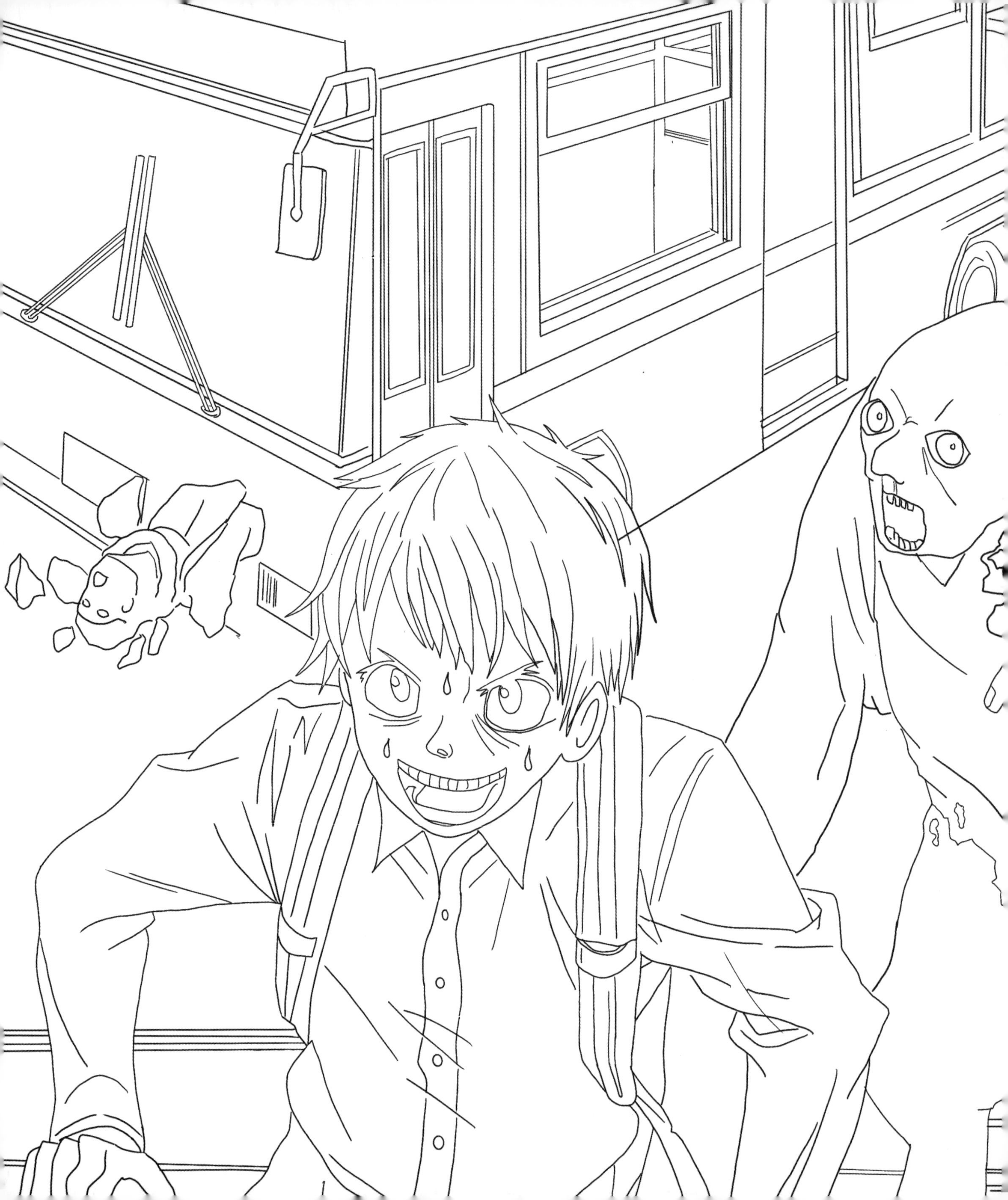

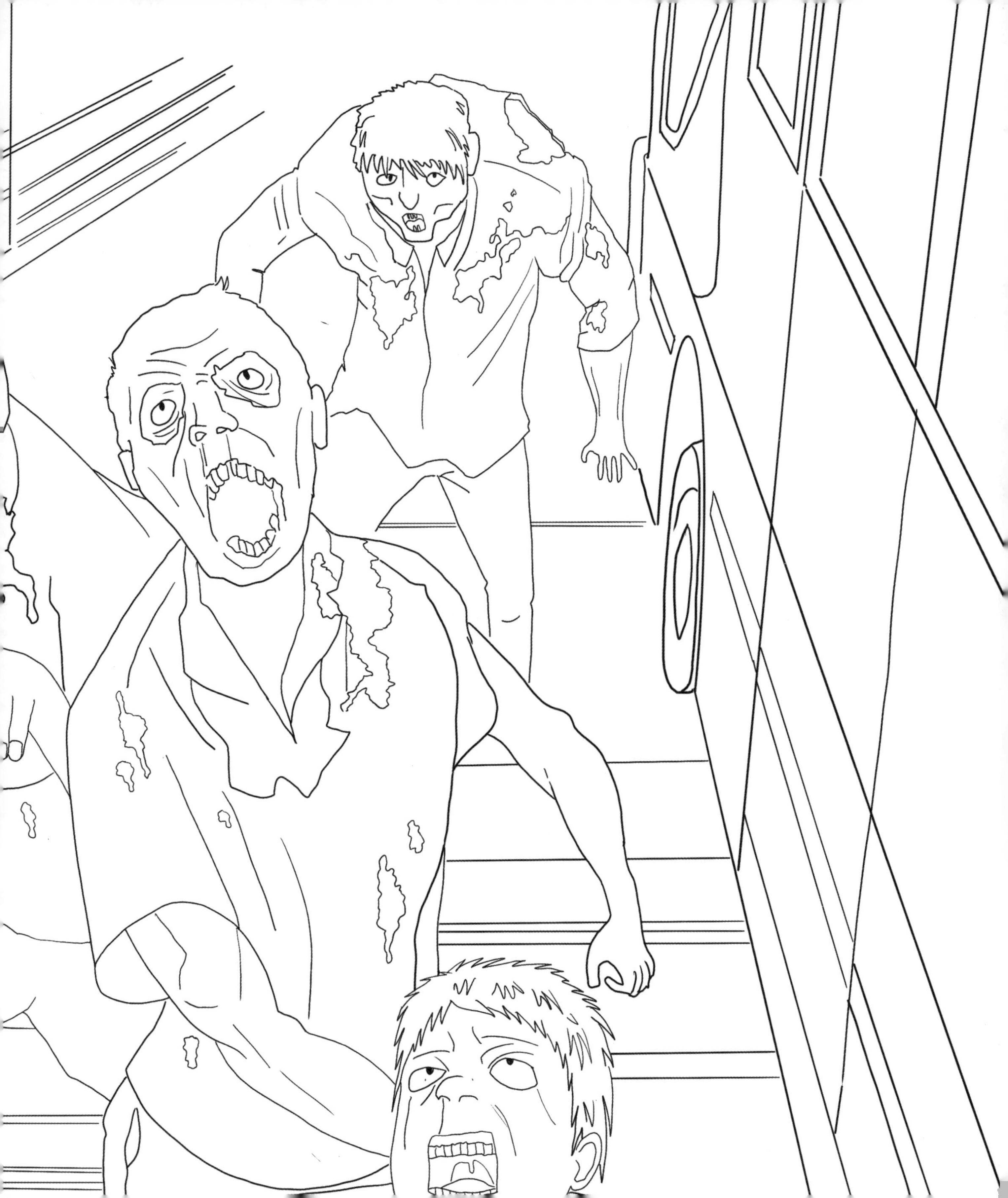

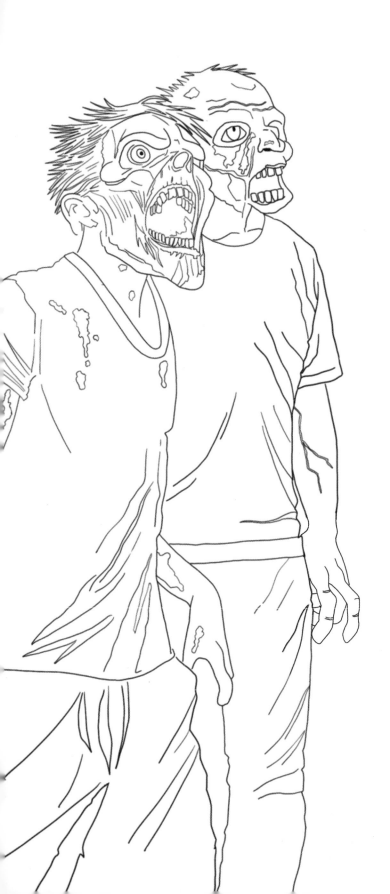

Quarto.com · WalterFoster.com

Copyright © 2024 Keo Media Ltd
Created and conceived by Keo Media Limited
www.keomedia.co.uk

Published in 2024 by Walter Foster Publishing,
an imprint of The Quarto Group,
100 Cummings Center, Suite 265D, Beverly, MA 01915, USA.
T (978) 282-9590 F (978) 283-2742

Walter Foster Publishing titles are also available at discount for retail, wholesale, promotional, and bulk purchase. For details, contact the Special Sales Manager by email at specialsales@quarto.com or by mail at The Quarto Group, Attn: Special Sales Manager, 100 Cummings Center, Suite 265D, Beverly, MA 01915, USA.

28 27 26 25 24   1 2 3 4 5

ISBN: 978-0-7603-9140-2

Creative Director: Siân Keogh
Editor: Anna Southgate
Designers: Sean Keogh
Production Director: Andy Cumming

Illustrations conceived and created by:
Creative-8 at PaperPlanitStudios

Printed in China